50 Premium Island Lunch Recipes for Home

By: Kelly Johnson

Table of Contents

- Grilled Mahi-Mahi Sandwiches
- Coconut-Curry Chicken Salad
- Island-Style Fish Tacos
- Jerk Chicken Wraps
- Pineapple and Shrimp Fried Rice
- Tropical BBQ Pulled Pork Sandwiches
- Caribbean Black Bean and Corn Salad
- Coconut-Lime Chicken Skewers
- Mango and Avocado Sushi Rolls
- Jamaican Beef Patties
- Tropical Tuna Poke Bowl
- Sweet and Spicy Pineapple Glazed Pork
- Grilled Veggie and Hummus Wraps
- Spicy Coconut Fish Stew
- Island-Style Chicken Quesadillas
- Coconut Curry Shrimp and Grits
- Tropical Chicken and Pineapple Skewers
- Papaya and Avocado Salad with Lime Vinaigrette
- Caribbean Jerk Beef Tacos
- Tropical Chicken Caesar Salad
- Coconut-Mango Shrimp Salad
- Island-Style Stuffed Bell Peppers
- Grilled Pineapple and Teriyaki Chicken Sandwiches
- Caribbean Fish and Chips
- Pineapple-Jalapeño Chicken Wraps
- Tropical Shrimp and Avocado Salad
- Coconut-Basil Chicken Bites
- Island-Style Turkey Burgers
- Mango-Coconut Chicken Stir-Fry
- Pineapple-Glazed Chicken Skewers
- Caribbean-Style Veggie Burger
- Tropical BBQ Chicken Salad

- Coconut and Pineapple Chicken Curry
- Island-Style Beef and Vegetable Stir-Fry
- Tropical Tuna Salad with Mango
- Grilled Coconut-Lime Chicken
- Jerk-Spiced Pulled Pork Tacos
- Pineapple and Avocado Chicken Wraps
- Coconut-Curry Beef Stew
- Tropical Fruit and Chicken Wraps
- Jamaican Jerk Chicken Salad
- Caribbean Pork and Pineapple Skewers
- Spicy Pineapple Shrimp Tacos
- Grilled Chicken and Mango Salsa Wraps
- Tropical Chicken and Rice Bowl
- Island-Style Crab Cakes
- Pineapple-Coconut Chicken Salad
- Caribbean Spiced Chicken Panini
- Tropical Fish Tacos with Avocado Sauce
- Pineapple and Ginger Chicken Stir-Fry

Grilled Mahi-Mahi Sandwiches

Ingredients:

For the Fish:

- 4 Mahi-Mahi fillets (6 oz each)
- 2 tbsp olive oil
- 1 tbsp lime juice
- 1 tsp paprika
- 1 tsp garlic powder
- 1/2 tsp ground cumin
- 1/2 tsp dried oregano
- Salt and pepper to taste

For the Sandwiches:

- 4 sandwich rolls or burger buns
- 1/2 cup mayonnaise
- 2 tbsp lime juice
- 1 tbsp chopped fresh cilantro
- 1 cup shredded lettuce
- 1 tomato, sliced
- 1 avocado, sliced
- Pickles (optional)
- Additional cilantro for garnish (optional)

Instructions:

1. **Prepare the Marinade:**
   - In a small bowl, mix together the olive oil, lime juice, paprika, garlic powder, cumin, oregano, salt, and pepper.
   - Rub the mixture evenly over the Mahi-Mahi fillets. Let the fish marinate for about 15-20 minutes.
2. **Grill the Fish:**
   - Preheat your grill to medium-high heat.
   - Grill the Mahi-Mahi fillets for about 4-5 minutes per side, or until the fish is cooked through and flakes easily with a fork. The internal temperature should reach 145°F (63°C).
3. **Prepare the Sauce:**
   - In a small bowl, combine the mayonnaise, lime juice, and chopped cilantro. Mix until well combined.
4. **Assemble the Sandwiches:**

- Toast the sandwich rolls or burger buns on the grill for about 1-2 minutes, or until lightly browned.
- Spread a generous amount of the lime-cilantro mayo on the bottom half of each roll.
- Top with shredded lettuce, a grilled Mahi-Mahi fillet, tomato slices, avocado slices, and pickles if using.
- Garnish with additional cilantro if desired.

5. **Serve:**
   - Place the top half of the roll on the sandwich and serve immediately.

Enjoy:

- Enjoy your delicious and refreshing Grilled Mahi-Mahi Sandwiches!

These sandwiches are perfect for a light and flavorful lunch with a tropical twist. The grilled Mahi-Mahi pairs beautifully with the zesty lime-cilantro mayo and fresh vegetables.

Coconut-Curry Chicken Salad

Ingredients:

- 2 cups cooked chicken breast, shredded or diced
- 1/2 cup shredded coconut
- 1/2 cup mayonnaise
- 1/4 cup plain Greek yogurt
- 2 tbsp curry powder
- 1 tbsp lime juice
- 1 tbsp honey
- 1/2 cup diced celery
- 1/2 cup diced apple
- 1/4 cup chopped red onion
- 1/4 cup chopped fresh cilantro (optional)
- Salt and pepper to taste

Instructions:

1. **Prepare the Dressing:**
    - In a large bowl, mix together the mayonnaise, Greek yogurt, curry powder, lime juice, and honey until well combined.
2. **Combine Ingredients:**
    - Add the shredded chicken, shredded coconut, diced celery, diced apple, red onion, and cilantro (if using) to the bowl with the dressing.
    - Gently fold the ingredients together until everything is evenly coated with the dressing.
3. **Season:**
    - Season with salt and pepper to taste. Mix well.
4. **Chill and Serve:**
    - Cover the bowl and refrigerate the chicken salad for at least 30 minutes to allow the flavors to meld.
    - Serve chilled on a bed of greens, in a sandwich, or with crackers.

Enjoy:

- Enjoy your creamy and flavorful Coconut-Curry Chicken Salad!

This salad combines the rich flavors of coconut and curry with a touch of sweetness from honey and apple, making it a deliciously unique and satisfying meal.

Island-Style Fish Tacos

Ingredients:

For the Fish:

- 1 lb white fish fillets (such as cod, tilapia, or mahi-mahi)
- 1/4 cup all-purpose flour
- 1/4 cup cornmeal
- 1 tsp paprika
- 1/2 tsp garlic powder
- 1/2 tsp ground cumin
- 1/2 tsp salt
- 1/4 tsp black pepper
- 1 egg
- 1/2 cup buttermilk or milk
- Vegetable oil for frying

For the Slaw:

- 2 cups shredded cabbage
- 1/2 cup shredded carrots
- 1/4 cup chopped fresh cilantro
- 2 tbsp lime juice
- 1 tbsp honey
- Salt and pepper to taste

For the Sauce:

- 1/2 cup sour cream
- 2 tbsp mayonnaise
- 1 tbsp lime juice
- 1 tbsp chopped fresh cilantro
- 1 tsp honey
- Salt and pepper to taste

To Serve:

- 8 small corn or flour tortillas
- Lime wedges
- Sliced avocado (optional)

Instructions:

1. **Prepare the Fish:**
    - In a shallow dish, mix the flour, cornmeal, paprika, garlic powder, cumin, salt, and pepper.
    - In another dish, whisk together the egg and buttermilk.
    - Dip each fish fillet into the egg mixture, then dredge in the flour mixture, coating evenly.
    - Heat vegetable oil in a large skillet over medium-high heat. Fry the fish fillets for about 3-4 minutes per side, or until golden brown and cooked through. Drain on paper towels.
2. **Prepare the Slaw:**
    - In a large bowl, combine the shredded cabbage, carrots, cilantro, lime juice, honey, salt, and pepper. Toss well to coat and set aside.
3. **Prepare the Sauce:**
    - In a small bowl, mix together the sour cream, mayonnaise, lime juice, cilantro, honey, salt, and pepper until smooth.
4. **Assemble the Tacos:**
    - Warm the tortillas in a dry skillet or in the oven.
    - Cut the cooked fish into bite-sized pieces.
    - Spread a small amount of sauce on each tortilla, then top with pieces of fish.
    - Add a generous amount of slaw on top of the fish.
5. **Serve:**
    - Garnish with lime wedges and sliced avocado if desired. Serve immediately.

Enjoy:

- Enjoy your flavorful and fresh Island-Style Fish Tacos!

These tacos offer a perfect blend of crispy fish, tangy slaw, and creamy sauce, with a vibrant island flair.

Jerk Chicken Wraps

Ingredients:

For the Jerk Chicken:

- 1 lb boneless, skinless chicken breasts or thighs
- 2 tbsp olive oil
- 2 tbsp jerk seasoning (store-bought or homemade, see below)
- 2 cloves garlic, minced
- 1 tbsp fresh lime juice
- 1 tbsp soy sauce
- 1 tbsp brown sugar
- 1/2 tsp ground allspice
- 1/2 tsp ground cinnamon

For the Wraps:

- 4 large flour tortillas or flatbreads
- 1 cup shredded lettuce
- 1/2 cup diced tomatoes
- 1/4 cup thinly sliced red onion
- 1/2 cup sliced avocado
- 1/2 cup shredded cheese (cheddar or a blend)
- 1/4 cup fresh cilantro, chopped

For the Jerk Seasoning (if making homemade):

- 1 tbsp allspice
- 1 tbsp paprika
- 1 tsp thyme
- 1 tsp garlic powder
- 1 tsp onion powder
- 1/2 tsp cayenne pepper (adjust to taste)
- 1/2 tsp ground ginger
- 1/2 tsp black pepper
- 1/2 tsp salt

For the Sauce (optional):

- 1/4 cup mayonnaise
- 1 tbsp lime juice
- 1 tbsp honey
- 1 tsp jerk seasoning

Instructions:

1. **Prepare the Jerk Chicken:**
   - In a small bowl, mix together the jerk seasoning, garlic, lime juice, soy sauce, brown sugar, allspice, and cinnamon.
   - Rub the mixture all over the chicken breasts or thighs. Let the chicken marinate for at least 30 minutes, or up to overnight in the refrigerator for deeper flavor.
   - Heat olive oil in a grill pan or skillet over medium-high heat. Cook the chicken for 6-7 minutes per side, or until fully cooked and the internal temperature reaches 165°F (74°C). Alternatively, you can grill the chicken for a smoky flavor.
   - Let the chicken rest for a few minutes before slicing into strips.
2. **Prepare the Wraps:**
   - If making the sauce, mix the mayonnaise, lime juice, honey, and jerk seasoning in a small bowl. Set aside.
   - Warm the tortillas or flatbreads in a dry skillet or microwave.
3. **Assemble the Wraps:**
   - Spread a thin layer of the optional sauce on each tortilla.
   - Lay down a bed of shredded lettuce in the center of each tortilla.
   - Top with slices of jerk chicken, diced tomatoes, red onion, avocado, and shredded cheese.
   - Sprinkle with fresh cilantro.
4. **Wrap and Serve:**
   - Fold in the sides of the tortilla, then roll up from the bottom to enclose the filling.
   - Cut in half if desired and serve immediately.

Enjoy:

- Enjoy your flavorful and spicy Jerk Chicken Wraps!

These wraps are a delicious and convenient way to enjoy the bold flavors of jerk chicken, perfect for a quick lunch or casual meal.

Pineapple and Shrimp Fried Rice

Ingredients:

For the Fish:

- 1 lb white fish fillets (such as cod, tilapia, or mahi-mahi)
- 1/4 cup all-purpose flour
- 1/4 cup cornmeal
- 1 tsp paprika
- 1/2 tsp garlic powder
- 1/2 tsp ground cumin
- 1/2 tsp salt
- 1/4 tsp black pepper
- 1 egg
- 1/2 cup buttermilk or milk
- Vegetable oil for frying

For the Slaw:

- 2 cups shredded cabbage
- 1/2 cup shredded carrots
- 1/4 cup chopped fresh cilantro
- 2 tbsp lime juice
- 1 tbsp honey
- Salt and pepper to taste

For the Sauce:

- 1/2 cup sour cream
- 2 tbsp mayonnaise
- 1 tbsp lime juice
- 1 tbsp chopped fresh cilantro
- 1 tsp honey
- Salt and pepper to taste

To Serve:

- 8 small corn or flour tortillas
- Lime wedges
- Sliced avocado (optional)

Instructions:

1. **Prepare the Fish:**
    - In a shallow dish, mix the flour, cornmeal, paprika, garlic powder, cumin, salt, and pepper.
    - In another dish, whisk together the egg and buttermilk.
    - Dip each fish fillet into the egg mixture, then dredge in the flour mixture, coating evenly.
    - Heat vegetable oil in a large skillet over medium-high heat. Fry the fish fillets for about 3-4 minutes per side, or until golden brown and cooked through. Drain on paper towels.
2. **Prepare the Slaw:**
    - In a large bowl, combine the shredded cabbage, carrots, cilantro, lime juice, honey, salt, and pepper. Toss well to coat and set aside.
3. **Prepare the Sauce:**
    - In a small bowl, mix together the sour cream, mayonnaise, lime juice, cilantro, honey, salt, and pepper until smooth.
4. **Assemble the Tacos:**
    - Warm the tortillas in a dry skillet or in the oven.
    - Cut the cooked fish into bite-sized pieces.
    - Spread a small amount of sauce on each tortilla, then top with pieces of fish.
    - Add a generous amount of slaw on top of the fish.
5. **Serve:**
    - Garnish with lime wedges and sliced avocado if desired. Serve immediately.

Enjoy:

- Enjoy your flavorful and fresh Island-Style Fish Tacos!

These tacos offer a perfect blend of crispy fish, tangy slaw, and creamy sauce, with a vibrant island flair.

Jerk Chicken Wraps

Ingredients:

For the Jerk Chicken:

- 1 lb boneless, skinless chicken breasts or thighs
- 2 tbsp olive oil
- 2 tbsp jerk seasoning (store-bought or homemade, see below)
- 2 cloves garlic, minced
- 1 tbsp fresh lime juice
- 1 tbsp soy sauce
- 1 tbsp brown sugar
- 1/2 tsp ground allspice
- 1/2 tsp ground cinnamon

For the Wraps:

- 4 large flour tortillas or flatbreads
- 1 cup shredded lettuce
- 1/2 cup diced tomatoes
- 1/4 cup thinly sliced red onion
- 1/2 cup sliced avocado
- 1/2 cup shredded cheese (cheddar or a blend)
- 1/4 cup fresh cilantro, chopped

For the Jerk Seasoning (if making homemade):

- 1 tbsp allspice
- 1 tbsp paprika
- 1 tsp thyme
- 1 tsp garlic powder
- 1 tsp onion powder
- 1/2 tsp cayenne pepper (adjust to taste)
- 1/2 tsp ground ginger
- 1/2 tsp black pepper
- 1/2 tsp salt

For the Sauce (optional):

- 1/4 cup mayonnaise
- 1 tbsp lime juice
- 1 tbsp honey
- 1 tsp jerk seasoning

Instructions:

1. **Prepare the Jerk Chicken:**
    - In a small bowl, mix together the jerk seasoning, garlic, lime juice, soy sauce, brown sugar, allspice, and cinnamon.
    - Rub the mixture all over the chicken breasts or thighs. Let the chicken marinate for at least 30 minutes, or up to overnight in the refrigerator for deeper flavor.
    - Heat olive oil in a grill pan or skillet over medium-high heat. Cook the chicken for 6-7 minutes per side, or until fully cooked and the internal temperature reaches 165°F (74°C). Alternatively, you can grill the chicken for a smoky flavor.
    - Let the chicken rest for a few minutes before slicing into strips.
2. **Prepare the Wraps:**
    - If making the sauce, mix the mayonnaise, lime juice, honey, and jerk seasoning in a small bowl. Set aside.
    - Warm the tortillas or flatbreads in a dry skillet or microwave.
3. **Assemble the Wraps:**
    - Spread a thin layer of the optional sauce on each tortilla.
    - Lay down a bed of shredded lettuce in the center of each tortilla.
    - Top with slices of jerk chicken, diced tomatoes, red onion, avocado, and shredded cheese.
    - Sprinkle with fresh cilantro.
4. **Wrap and Serve:**
    - Fold in the sides of the tortilla, then roll up from the bottom to enclose the filling.
    - Cut in half if desired and serve immediately.

Enjoy:

- Enjoy your flavorful and spicy Jerk Chicken Wraps!

These wraps are a delicious and convenient way to enjoy the bold flavors of jerk chicken, perfect for a quick lunch or casual meal.

Jerk Chicken Wraps

Ingredients:

For the Jerk Chicken:

- 1 lb boneless, skinless chicken breasts or thighs
- 2 tbsp olive oil
- 2 tbsp jerk seasoning (store-bought or homemade, see below)
- 2 cloves garlic, minced
- 1 tbsp fresh lime juice
- 1 tbsp soy sauce
- 1 tbsp brown sugar
- 1/2 tsp ground allspice
- 1/2 tsp ground cinnamon

For the Wraps:

- 4 large flour tortillas or flatbreads
- 1 cup shredded lettuce
- 1/2 cup diced tomatoes
- 1/4 cup thinly sliced red onion
- 1/2 cup sliced avocado
- 1/2 cup shredded cheese (cheddar or a blend)
- 1/4 cup fresh cilantro, chopped

For the Jerk Seasoning (if making homemade):

- 1 tbsp allspice
- 1 tbsp paprika
- 1 tsp thyme
- 1 tsp garlic powder
- 1 tsp onion powder
- 1/2 tsp cayenne pepper (adjust to taste)
- 1/2 tsp ground ginger
- 1/2 tsp black pepper
- 1/2 tsp salt

For the Sauce (optional):

- 1/4 cup mayonnaise
- 1 tbsp lime juice
- 1 tbsp honey
- 1 tsp jerk seasoning

Instructions:

1. **Prepare the Jerk Chicken:**
    - In a small bowl, mix together the jerk seasoning, garlic, lime juice, soy sauce, brown sugar, allspice, and cinnamon.
    - Rub the mixture all over the chicken breasts or thighs. Let the chicken marinate for at least 30 minutes, or up to overnight in the refrigerator for deeper flavor.
    - Heat olive oil in a grill pan or skillet over medium-high heat. Cook the chicken for 6-7 minutes per side, or until fully cooked and the internal temperature reaches 165°F (74°C). Alternatively, you can grill the chicken for a smoky flavor.
    - Let the chicken rest for a few minutes before slicing into strips.
2. **Prepare the Wraps:**
    - If making the sauce, mix the mayonnaise, lime juice, honey, and jerk seasoning in a small bowl. Set aside.
    - Warm the tortillas or flatbreads in a dry skillet or microwave.
3. **Assemble the Wraps:**
    - Spread a thin layer of the optional sauce on each tortilla.
    - Lay down a bed of shredded lettuce in the center of each tortilla.
    - Top with slices of jerk chicken, diced tomatoes, red onion, avocado, and shredded cheese.
    - Sprinkle with fresh cilantro.
4. **Wrap and Serve:**
    - Fold in the sides of the tortilla, then roll up from the bottom to enclose the filling.
    - Cut in half if desired and serve immediately.

Enjoy:

- Enjoy your flavorful and spicy Jerk Chicken Wraps!

These wraps are a delicious and convenient way to enjoy the bold flavors of jerk chicken, perfect for a quick lunch or casual meal.

Pineapple and Shrimp Fried Rice

Ingredients:

- 2 cups cooked jasmine rice (preferably cold or day-old for best results)
- 1/2 lb shrimp, peeled and deveined
- 1 cup fresh pineapple, diced
- 2 tbsp vegetable oil
- 1/2 cup diced onion
- 1/2 cup diced bell pepper (red or yellow)
- 2 cloves garlic, minced
- 1/2 cup frozen peas and carrots mix
- 2 large eggs, lightly beaten
- 3 tbsp soy sauce
- 1 tbsp oyster sauce (optional)
- 1 tsp sesame oil
- 2 green onions, sliced
- 1/4 cup chopped fresh cilantro (optional)
- Salt and pepper to taste

Instructions:

1. **Prepare the Shrimp:**
    - In a large skillet or wok, heat 1 tablespoon of vegetable oil over medium-high heat.
    - Add the shrimp and cook for about 2-3 minutes per side, or until pink and cooked through. Remove shrimp from the skillet and set aside.
2. **Cook the Vegetables:**
    - In the same skillet, add the remaining tablespoon of vegetable oil.
    - Sauté the diced onion and bell pepper until they begin to soften, about 3-4 minutes.
    - Add the minced garlic and cook for another 30 seconds until fragrant.
    - Stir in the frozen peas and carrots, and cook for an additional 2 minutes.
3. **Scramble the Eggs:**
    - Push the vegetables to one side of the skillet. Pour the beaten eggs into the empty side and scramble until fully cooked. Combine with the vegetables.
4. **Fry the Rice:**
    - Add the cold rice to the skillet, breaking up any clumps. Stir to combine with the vegetables and eggs.
    - Add the diced pineapple and cooked shrimp back into the skillet. Stir well to combine all ingredients.
5. **Season the Rice:**

- Pour the soy sauce, oyster sauce (if using), and sesame oil over the rice. Stir until the rice is evenly coated and heated through. Season with salt and pepper to taste.
6. **Finish and Serve:**
    - Stir in the sliced green onions and chopped cilantro, if using.
    - Serve hot.

Enjoy:

- Enjoy your tropical Pineapple and Shrimp Fried Rice!

This dish combines the sweetness of pineapple with the savory flavors of shrimp and fried rice, making for a vibrant and satisfying meal.

Tropical BBQ Pulled Pork Sandwiches

Ingredients:

For the Pulled Pork:

- 3-4 lbs pork shoulder (also known as pork butt)
- 1 tbsp olive oil
- 1 onion, chopped
- 3 cloves garlic, minced
- 1 cup pineapple juice
- 1/2 cup BBQ sauce (use your favorite brand)
- 1/4 cup soy sauce
- 1/4 cup apple cider vinegar
- 2 tbsp brown sugar
- 1 tsp ground cumin
- 1 tsp smoked paprika
- 1/2 tsp ground cinnamon
- 1/2 tsp salt
- 1/4 tsp black pepper

For the Slaw:

- 2 cups shredded cabbage
- 1/2 cup shredded carrots
- 1/4 cup chopped fresh cilantro
- 1/4 cup pineapple chunks (fresh or canned)
- 2 tbsp lime juice
- 1 tbsp honey
- Salt and pepper to taste

To Serve:

- 8 sandwich rolls or buns
- Pickles (optional)
- Sliced jalapeños (optional)

Instructions:

1. **Prepare the Pulled Pork:**
    - Heat the olive oil in a large skillet or Dutch oven over medium-high heat. Sear the pork shoulder on all sides until browned, about 4-5 minutes per side. Transfer to a slow cooker or a large baking dish.

- In the same skillet, add the chopped onion and cook until softened, about 3 minutes. Add the minced garlic and cook for another 30 seconds.
- Pour in the pineapple juice, BBQ sauce, soy sauce, apple cider vinegar, brown sugar, cumin, smoked paprika, cinnamon, salt, and pepper. Stir to combine.
- Pour the mixture over the pork shoulder in the slow cooker or baking dish.

2. **Slow Cook or Bake the Pork:**
   - **Slow Cooker Method:** Cover and cook on low for 8 hours, or until the pork is tender and easily shreds with a fork.
   - **Oven Method:** Preheat the oven to 300°F (150°C). Cover the baking dish with aluminum foil and bake for 4-5 hours, or until the pork is tender and easily shreds.

3. **Shred the Pork:**
   - Remove the pork shoulder from the cooking liquid and shred it using two forks. Return the shredded pork to the cooking liquid and stir to combine.

4. **Prepare the Slaw:**
   - In a large bowl, combine the shredded cabbage, shredded carrots, chopped cilantro, pineapple chunks, lime juice, and honey. Toss well to coat.
   - Season with salt and pepper to taste.

5. **Assemble the Sandwiches:**
   - Toast the sandwich rolls or buns lightly, if desired.
   - Pile a generous amount of pulled pork onto the bottom half of each roll.
   - Top with a portion of the pineapple slaw.
   - Add pickles and sliced jalapeños if desired.

6. **Serve:**
   - Place the top half of the roll on the sandwich and serve immediately.

Enjoy:

- Enjoy your delicious Tropical BBQ Pulled Pork Sandwiches!

These sandwiches offer a perfect blend of sweet and tangy flavors with a tropical twist, making them a great choice for a satisfying and flavorful meal.

Caribbean Black Bean and Corn Salad

Ingredients:

- 1 can (15 oz) black beans, drained and rinsed
- 1 cup frozen corn kernels, thawed
- 1 red bell pepper, diced
- 1/2 cup red onion, finely chopped
- 1/2 cup cherry tomatoes, halved
- 1 avocado, diced
- 1/4 cup fresh cilantro, chopped
- 1/4 cup lime juice (about 2 limes)
- 2 tbsp olive oil
- 1 tbsp honey
- 1 tsp ground cumin
- 1/2 tsp paprika
- Salt and pepper to taste

Instructions:

1. **Prepare the Vegetables:**
   - In a large bowl, combine the black beans, corn, red bell pepper, red onion, cherry tomatoes, and avocado.
2. **Make the Dressing:**
   - In a small bowl, whisk together the lime juice, olive oil, honey, ground cumin, paprika, salt, and pepper until well combined.
3. **Combine:**
   - Pour the dressing over the vegetable mixture and toss gently to coat.
4. **Add Cilantro:**
   - Stir in the chopped fresh cilantro.
5. **Chill and Serve:**
   - Cover the salad and refrigerate for at least 30 minutes to allow the flavors to meld.
   - Serve chilled or at room temperature.

Enjoy:

- Enjoy your vibrant and refreshing Caribbean Black Bean and Corn Salad!

This salad offers a delightful mix of textures and flavors with a zesty dressing that complements the ingredients perfectly.

Coconut-Lime Chicken Skewers

Ingredients:

For the Marinade:

- 1 cup coconut milk (full-fat or light)
- 1/4 cup fresh lime juice (about 2 limes)
- 2 tbsp soy sauce
- 2 tbsp honey
- 2 cloves garlic, minced
- 1 tbsp fresh ginger, minced
- 1 tsp ground cumin
- 1/2 tsp ground coriander
- 1/2 tsp paprika
- Salt and pepper to taste

For the Skewers:

- 1.5 lbs boneless, skinless chicken breasts or thighs, cut into bite-sized pieces
- Wooden or metal skewers (if using wooden skewers, soak in water for 30 minutes before using)

For Garnish (optional):

- Fresh cilantro, chopped
- Lime wedges

Instructions:

1. **Prepare the Marinade:**
    - In a bowl, combine the coconut milk, lime juice, soy sauce, honey, minced garlic, minced ginger, ground cumin, ground coriander, paprika, salt, and pepper. Whisk until well combined.
2. **Marinate the Chicken:**
    - Place the chicken pieces in a resealable plastic bag or a shallow dish.
    - Pour the marinade over the chicken and toss to coat.
    - Seal the bag or cover the dish and refrigerate for at least 1 hour, or up to 4 hours for more flavor.
3. **Prepare the Skewers:**
    - Preheat your grill to medium-high heat.
    - Thread the marinated chicken pieces onto the skewers, leaving a little space between each piece.
4. **Grill the Skewers:**

- Place the skewers on the grill and cook for about 4-5 minutes per side, or until the chicken is cooked through and has nice grill marks. The internal temperature should reach 165°F (74°C).
5. **Garnish and Serve:**
    - Remove the skewers from the grill and let them rest for a few minutes.
    - Garnish with chopped fresh cilantro and serve with lime wedges on the side.

Enjoy:

- Enjoy your flavorful and tropical Coconut-Lime Chicken Skewers!

These skewers are perfect for a light yet satisfying meal, offering a delicious combination of coconut and lime with grilled chicken.

Mango and Avocado Sushi Rolls

Ingredients:

For the Sushi Rice:

- 1 1/2 cups sushi rice
- 2 cups water
- 1/3 cup rice vinegar
- 3 tbsp sugar
- 1 tsp salt

For the Sushi Rolls:

- 1 ripe mango, peeled, pitted, and sliced into thin strips
- 1 ripe avocado, sliced into thin strips
- 4 sheets nori (seaweed)
- 1/2 cucumber, peeled and sliced into thin strips (optional)
- Soy sauce, for dipping
- Pickled ginger, for serving (optional)
- Wasabi, for serving (optional)

Equipment:

- Bamboo sushi mat (covered with plastic wrap)
- Sharp knife
- Rice paddle or spoon

Instructions:

1. **Prepare the Sushi Rice:**
    - Rinse the sushi rice under cold water until the water runs clear. This helps remove excess starch.
    - In a rice cooker or pot, combine the rinsed rice and water. Cook according to the rice cooker's instructions or bring to a boil, then reduce heat to low, cover, and simmer for 20 minutes. Let the rice sit covered for an additional 10 minutes off the heat.
    - In a small saucepan, heat the rice vinegar, sugar, and salt over low heat until the sugar and salt are dissolved. Let cool slightly.
    - Gently fold the vinegar mixture into the cooked rice using a rice paddle or spoon. Allow the rice to cool to room temperature.
2. **Assemble the Sushi Rolls:**
    - Place a sheet of nori on the bamboo sushi mat, shiny side down.

- Wet your hands to prevent sticking and spread a thin layer of sushi rice over the nori, leaving a 1-inch border at the top edge.
- Arrange a few strips of mango, avocado, and cucumber (if using) horizontally across the center of the rice.
3. **Roll the Sushi:**
    - Using the bamboo mat, carefully lift the edge of the nori closest to you and start rolling it over the filling, pressing gently to form a tight roll.
    - Continue rolling until you reach the exposed edge of the nori. Wet the edge of the nori with a little water and press to seal the roll.
4. **Slice the Sushi Rolls:**
    - Using a sharp knife, slice the roll into bite-sized pieces. To avoid sticking, lightly wet the knife between cuts.
5. **Serve:**
    - Arrange the sushi rolls on a serving platter.
    - Serve with soy sauce, pickled ginger, and wasabi on the side.

Enjoy:

- Enjoy your fresh and vibrant Mango and Avocado Sushi Rolls!

These sushi rolls are a refreshing and delicious combination of sweet mango and creamy avocado, making them a great choice for a light meal or appetizer.

Jamaican Beef Patties

Ingredients:

For the Filling:

- 1 lb ground beef
- 1 tbsp vegetable oil
- 1 medium onion, finely chopped
- 2 cloves garlic, minced
- 1 bell pepper (red or green), finely chopped
- 1 tbsp allspice
- 1 tsp paprika
- 1/2 tsp turmeric
- 1/2 tsp cayenne pepper (adjust to taste)
- 1/2 tsp thyme (dried or fresh)
- 1/2 cup beef or chicken broth
- 1/2 cup breadcrumbs
- 1 tbsp soy sauce
- Salt and pepper to taste

For the Dough:

- 2 1/2 cups all-purpose flour
- 1/2 tsp salt
- 1/2 tsp turmeric (for color)
- 1/2 cup unsalted butter, chilled and cut into small pieces
- 1/3 cup cold water
- 1 large egg, beaten (for egg wash)

Instructions:

1. **Prepare the Filling:**
    - Heat vegetable oil in a large skillet over medium heat.
    - Add the finely chopped onion, bell pepper, and garlic. Cook until softened, about 5 minutes.
    - Add the ground beef and cook until browned, breaking it up with a spoon as it cooks.
    - Stir in the allspice, paprika, turmeric, cayenne pepper, thyme, and salt and pepper. Cook for another 2 minutes.
    - Add the beef broth and breadcrumbs. Stir to combine and cook until the mixture thickens and most of the liquid is absorbed. Remove from heat and let cool.
2. **Prepare the Dough:**
    - In a large bowl, combine the flour, salt, and turmeric.

- Cut in the chilled butter using a pastry cutter or your fingers until the mixture resembles coarse crumbs.
- Gradually add the cold water, mixing until the dough comes together. You may need a little more or less water, so add it slowly.
- Form the dough into a ball, cover with plastic wrap, and refrigerate for at least 30 minutes.

3. **Assemble the Patties:**
   - Preheat your oven to 375°F (190°C).
   - On a lightly floured surface, roll out the dough to about 1/8 inch thickness.
   - Cut out circles using a 4-inch round cutter or a cup.
   - Place a spoonful of the cooled beef filling in the center of each dough circle.
   - Fold the dough over the filling to form a half-moon shape. Press the edges together with a fork to seal.

4. **Bake the Patties:**
   - Place the patties on a baking sheet lined with parchment paper.
   - Brush the tops of the patties with the beaten egg for a golden finish.
   - Bake in the preheated oven for 25-30 minutes, or until the patties are golden brown.

5. **Serve:**
   - Let the patties cool slightly before serving.

Enjoy:

- Enjoy your delicious homemade Jamaican Beef Patties!

These patties are perfect for a flavorful snack or meal, featuring a spicy beef filling encased in a flaky, golden crust.

Tropical Tuna Poke Bowl

Ingredients:

For the Tuna:

- 1 lb sushi-grade tuna, diced
- 2 tbsp soy sauce
- 1 tbsp sesame oil
- 1 tbsp rice vinegar
- 1 tsp honey
- 1/2 tsp grated ginger
- 1/2 tsp sesame seeds

For the Bowl:

- 2 cups cooked jasmine rice or sushi rice, cooled
- 1 cup diced mango
- 1 avocado, diced
- 1/2 cup cucumber, sliced
- 1/4 cup shredded carrots
- 1/4 cup edamame, cooked
- 1/4 cup thinly sliced radishes (optional)
- 2 tbsp chopped fresh cilantro
- 1 tbsp sliced green onions
- Pickled ginger, for garnish (optional)
- Soy sauce or ponzu sauce, for drizzling
- Sriracha or spicy mayo (optional, for a kick)

Instructions:

1. **Prepare the Tuna:**
    - In a bowl, combine the soy sauce, sesame oil, rice vinegar, honey, grated ginger, and sesame seeds.
    - Add the diced tuna and gently toss to coat. Let marinate for 10-15 minutes in the refrigerator.
2. **Assemble the Bowls:**
    - Divide the cooked rice evenly between bowls.
    - Arrange the marinated tuna, mango, avocado, cucumber, shredded carrots, edamame, and radishes (if using) on top of the rice.
3. **Garnish and Serve:**
    - Sprinkle with chopped cilantro and sliced green onions.
    - Drizzle with soy sauce or ponzu sauce. Add pickled ginger and a dollop of sriracha or spicy mayo if desired.

Enjoy:

- Enjoy your refreshing and vibrant Tropical Tuna Poke Bowl!

This dish combines the freshness of tropical fruits with the savory flavors of tuna, making for a delicious and visually appealing meal.

Sweet and Spicy Pineapple Glazed Pork

Ingredients:

For the Pork:

- 1.5 to 2 lbs pork tenderloin or pork chops
- 2 tbsp olive oil
- Salt and black pepper to taste

For the Pineapple Glaze:

- 1 cup pineapple juice
- 1/4 cup soy sauce
- 1/4 cup honey
- 2 tbsp brown sugar
- 2 tbsp rice vinegar
- 1 tbsp sriracha or hot sauce (adjust to taste)
- 2 cloves garlic, minced
- 1 tbsp fresh ginger, minced
- 1 tbsp cornstarch mixed with 2 tbsp water (for thickening)
- 1 tbsp sesame seeds (optional, for garnish)
- 2 green onions, sliced (optional, for garnish)

Instructions:

1. **Prepare the Pork:**
    - Preheat your oven to 375°F (190°C) if using pork tenderloin.
    - Season the pork with salt and black pepper.
    - Heat olive oil in a large skillet over medium-high heat.
    - Sear the pork on all sides until golden brown, about 2-3 minutes per side.
    - Transfer the pork to a baking dish and roast in the preheated oven for 20-25 minutes, or until the internal temperature reaches 145°F (63°C). (For pork chops, cook according to thickness, usually 10-15 minutes.)
2. **Make the Pineapple Glaze:**
    - In a saucepan, combine pineapple juice, soy sauce, honey, brown sugar, rice vinegar, sriracha, minced garlic, and minced ginger.
    - Bring to a boil over medium-high heat, then reduce to a simmer and cook for about 5 minutes.
    - Stir in the cornstarch mixture and continue to cook until the glaze thickens, about 2-3 minutes.
3. **Glaze the Pork:**
    - Once the pork is cooked, remove it from the oven and let it rest for 5 minutes.
    - Slice the pork into medallions and brush with the pineapple glaze.

4. **Serve:**
    - Drizzle additional glaze over the sliced pork.
    - Garnish with sesame seeds and sliced green onions, if desired.

Enjoy:

- Enjoy your Sweet and Spicy Pineapple Glazed Pork!

This dish offers a delightful balance of sweet and spicy flavors with a tangy pineapple glaze that complements the pork perfectly.

Grilled Veggie and Hummus Wraps

Ingredients:

For the Wraps:

- 4 large whole wheat or flour tortillas
- 1 medium zucchini, sliced
- 1 red bell pepper, sliced
- 1 yellow bell pepper, sliced
- 1 cup mushrooms, sliced
- 1 red onion, sliced
- 2 tbsp olive oil
- Salt and black pepper to taste
- 1/2 tsp dried oregano or Italian seasoning
- 1/2 cup hummus (store-bought or homemade)
- 1 cup baby spinach or mixed greens
- 1 avocado, sliced (optional)

For Homemade Hummus (optional):

- 1 can (15 oz) chickpeas, drained and rinsed
- 1/4 cup tahini
- 1/4 cup lemon juice (about 1 lemon)
- 1 garlic clove
- 2 tbsp olive oil
- Salt to taste
- Water, as needed for consistency

Instructions:

1. **Prepare the Veggies:**
   - Preheat your grill or grill pan to medium-high heat.
   - Toss the zucchini, red bell pepper, yellow bell pepper, mushrooms, and red onion with olive oil, salt, black pepper, and dried oregano.
   - Grill the vegetables for about 5-7 minutes per side, or until they are tender and have grill marks. Remove from heat and set aside.
2. **Prepare the Hummus (if making homemade):**
   - In a food processor, combine chickpeas, tahini, lemon juice, garlic, olive oil, and salt.
   - Process until smooth, adding water a tablespoon at a time to reach your desired consistency.
3. **Assemble the Wraps:**
   - Spread a generous layer of hummus over each tortilla.

- Layer the grilled vegetables evenly on top of the hummus.
- Add a handful of baby spinach or mixed greens and avocado slices (if using).
4. **Wrap and Serve:**
    - Roll up each tortilla tightly, folding in the sides as you go.
    - Slice the wraps in half diagonally and serve.

Enjoy:

- Enjoy your Grilled Veggie and Hummus Wraps!

These wraps are a great way to enjoy a healthy and satisfying meal with a delicious combination of grilled veggies and creamy hummus. They're perfect for lunch or a light dinner.

Spicy Coconut Fish Stew

Ingredients:

- 1 lb firm white fish (like cod or snapper), cut into chunks
- 2 tbsp vegetable oil
- 1 onion, finely chopped
- 2 cloves garlic, minced
- 1 red bell pepper, chopped
- 1 green bell pepper, chopped
- 1 tbsp fresh ginger, minced
- 1-2 hot chili peppers, sliced (adjust to taste)
- 1 can (14 oz) coconut milk
- 1 cup fish or vegetable broth
- 1 can (14.5 oz) diced tomatoes
- 1 tbsp curry powder
- 1 tsp ground turmeric
- 1 tsp paprika
- 1 tsp ground cumin
- 1/2 tsp salt (or to taste)
- 1/2 tsp black pepper (or to taste)
- 1 cup baby spinach or kale (optional)
- 2 tbsp fresh cilantro, chopped (for garnish)
- Lime wedges (for serving)

Instructions:

1. **Sauté the Aromatics:**
    - Heat vegetable oil in a large pot over medium heat.
    - Add the chopped onion and cook until translucent, about 5 minutes.
    - Stir in the garlic, ginger, and chili peppers, and cook for another 1-2 minutes until fragrant.
2. **Add Vegetables and Spices:**
    - Add the bell peppers and cook for an additional 3-4 minutes.
    - Stir in the curry powder, turmeric, paprika, cumin, salt, and black pepper, cooking for 1 minute to toast the spices.
3. **Add Liquids and Simmer:**
    - Pour in the coconut milk, fish or vegetable broth, and diced tomatoes.
    - Bring to a simmer and cook for 10 minutes to allow the flavors to meld.
4. **Cook the Fish:**
    - Gently add the fish chunks to the pot.
    - Simmer for about 5-7 minutes, or until the fish is cooked through and flakes easily.

5. **Add Greens (Optional):**
    - Stir in the baby spinach or kale, if using, and cook for an additional 1-2 minutes until wilted.
6. **Serve:**
    - Ladle the stew into bowls and garnish with fresh cilantro.
    - Serve with lime wedges on the side for a tangy finish.

Enjoy:

- Enjoy your Spicy Coconut Fish Stew!

This stew combines the richness of coconut milk with spicy and aromatic flavors, making it a hearty and satisfying dish.

Island-Style Chicken Quesadillas

Ingredients:

For the Chicken Filling:

- 1 lb boneless, skinless chicken breasts, cooked and shredded
- 1 tbsp olive oil
- 1 small onion, finely chopped
- 1 red bell pepper, chopped
- 2 cloves garlic, minced
- 1/2 cup pineapple chunks (fresh or canned, drained)
- 1/2 cup shredded cheddar cheese
- 1/2 cup shredded mozzarella cheese
- 1 tbsp soy sauce
- 1 tbsp honey
- 1/2 tsp ground cumin
- 1/2 tsp paprika
- 1/2 tsp dried thyme
- Salt and black pepper to taste

For the Quesadillas:

- 4 large flour tortillas
- 2 tbsp olive oil or butter (for cooking the quesadillas)

For Serving:

- Salsa or pico de gallo
- Sour cream
- Fresh cilantro, chopped
- Lime wedges

Instructions:

1. **Prepare the Chicken Filling:**
    - Heat olive oil in a large skillet over medium heat.
    - Add the chopped onion and bell pepper. Cook until softened, about 5 minutes.
    - Stir in the garlic and cook for another 1 minute.
    - Add the shredded chicken, pineapple chunks, soy sauce, honey, cumin, paprika, thyme, salt, and pepper. Stir to combine and cook for 3-4 minutes until heated through and well combined.
    - Remove from heat and let cool slightly.
2. **Assemble the Quesadillas:**

- Heat a large skillet or griddle over medium heat.
- Place one tortilla in the skillet and sprinkle with a portion of cheddar and mozzarella cheese.
- Spread a quarter of the chicken filling evenly over half of the tortilla.
- Fold the tortilla in half over the filling.
3. **Cook the Quesadillas:**
    - Cook the quesadilla for 2-3 minutes on each side, or until golden brown and the cheese is melted. Press down gently with a spatula to ensure even cooking.
    - Remove from the skillet and let cool slightly before slicing into wedges.
4. **Serve:**
    - Serve the quesadillas with salsa or pico de gallo, sour cream, chopped cilantro, and lime wedges on the side.

Enjoy:

- Enjoy your delicious Island-Style Chicken Quesadillas!

These quesadillas combine tropical flavors with classic quesadilla comfort, making them a fun and flavorful meal.

Coconut Curry Shrimp and Grits

Ingredients:

For the Shrimp:

- 1 lb large shrimp, peeled and deveined
- 1 tbsp olive oil
- 1 small onion, finely chopped
- 2 cloves garlic, minced
- 1 tbsp curry powder
- 1/2 tsp ground turmeric
- 1/2 tsp paprika
- 1/2 tsp cayenne pepper (adjust to taste)
- 1 can (14 oz) coconut milk
- 1/2 cup chicken or vegetable broth
- 1 tbsp lime juice
- Salt and black pepper to taste
- 2 tbsp chopped fresh cilantro (for garnish)

For the Grits:

- 1 cup grits (stone-ground or quick-cooking)
- 4 cups water or chicken broth
- 1 cup shredded cheddar cheese
- 2 tbsp butter
- Salt and black pepper to taste

Instructions:

1. **Prepare the Grits:**
   - In a medium saucepan, bring the water or chicken broth to a boil.
   - Gradually stir in the grits, reduce heat to low, and simmer, stirring occasionally, until the grits are tender and thickened (about 5-10 minutes for quick-cooking or 20-30 minutes for stone-ground).
   - Stir in the cheddar cheese and butter. Season with salt and black pepper. Keep warm.
2. **Prepare the Shrimp:**
   - Heat olive oil in a large skillet over medium heat.
   - Add the chopped onion and cook until translucent, about 5 minutes.
   - Stir in the garlic and cook for an additional 1 minute.
   - Add the curry powder, turmeric, paprika, and cayenne pepper, and cook for 1-2 minutes to toast the spices.

- Add the shrimp and cook for about 2-3 minutes per side, until pink and cooked through.
- Pour in the coconut milk and chicken or vegetable broth, and bring to a simmer. Cook for another 5 minutes, or until the sauce has slightly thickened.
- Stir in the lime juice and season with salt and black pepper.
3. **Serve:**
    - Spoon the grits onto plates or bowls.
    - Top with the coconut curry shrimp and sauce.
    - Garnish with chopped cilantro.

Enjoy:

- Enjoy your Coconut Curry Shrimp and Grits!

This dish combines creamy, cheesy grits with a rich, flavorful coconut curry sauce, creating a comforting and tropical meal.

Tropical Chicken and Pineapple Skewers

Ingredients:

For the Marinade:

- 1/4 cup soy sauce
- 2 tbsp honey
- 2 tbsp lime juice
- 2 tbsp olive oil
- 2 cloves garlic, minced
- 1 tsp grated fresh ginger
- 1/2 tsp ground cumin
- 1/2 tsp paprika
- 1/4 tsp red pepper flakes (optional, for heat)
- Salt and black pepper to taste

For the Skewers:

- 1.5 lbs boneless, skinless chicken breasts, cut into 1-inch cubes
- 1 cup pineapple chunks (fresh or canned, drained)
- 1 red bell pepper, cut into 1-inch pieces
- 1 green bell pepper, cut into 1-inch pieces
- 1 small red onion, cut into 1-inch pieces
- Fresh cilantro, chopped (for garnish)
- Lime wedges (for serving)

Instructions:

1. **Prepare the Marinade:**
    - In a bowl, whisk together soy sauce, honey, lime juice, olive oil, garlic, ginger, cumin, paprika, red pepper flakes, salt, and black pepper.
2. **Marinate the Chicken:**
    - Place the chicken cubes in a large zip-top bag or bowl.
    - Pour the marinade over the chicken and toss to coat.
    - Seal the bag or cover the bowl and refrigerate for at least 30 minutes, or up to 2 hours for more flavor.
3. **Assemble the Skewers:**
    - Preheat your grill to medium-high heat.
    - Thread the marinated chicken, pineapple chunks, red bell pepper, green bell pepper, and red onion onto skewers, alternating the ingredients.
4. **Grill the Skewers:**
    - Brush the grill grates with oil to prevent sticking.

- Place the skewers on the grill and cook for about 3-4 minutes per side, or until the chicken is cooked through and has nice grill marks. The pineapple should be slightly caramelized and the vegetables tender.
5. **Serve:**
    - Remove the skewers from the grill and garnish with chopped fresh cilantro.
    - Serve with lime wedges on the side.

Enjoy:

- Enjoy your Tropical Chicken and Pineapple Skewers!

These skewers offer a delicious blend of sweet pineapple, savory chicken, and vibrant vegetables, perfect for a tropical-inspired meal.

Papaya and Avocado Salad with Lime Vinaigrette

Ingredients:

For the Salad:

- 1 ripe papaya, peeled, seeded, and cubed
- 1 ripe avocado, peeled, pitted, and sliced
- 4 cups mixed greens (e.g., arugula, spinach, or baby kale)
- 1/4 cup red onion, thinly sliced
- 1/4 cup chopped fresh cilantro
- 1/4 cup crumbled feta cheese (optional)
- 1/4 cup toasted pumpkin seeds or sunflower seeds (optional, for crunch)

For the Lime Vinaigrette:

- 1/4 cup fresh lime juice (about 2 limes)
- 2 tbsp extra virgin olive oil
- 1 tbsp honey or agave syrup
- 1 clove garlic, minced
- 1/2 tsp ground cumin
- Salt and black pepper to taste

Instructions:

1. **Prepare the Lime Vinaigrette:**
    - In a small bowl or jar, whisk together the lime juice, olive oil, honey, minced garlic, and ground cumin.
    - Season with salt and black pepper to taste.
    - Adjust sweetness or acidity as needed. Set aside.
2. **Assemble the Salad:**
    - In a large salad bowl, combine the mixed greens, papaya cubes, avocado slices, and red onion.
    - Gently toss to mix, being careful not to mash the avocado.
3. **Add the Vinaigrette:**
    - Drizzle the lime vinaigrette over the salad.
    - Toss gently to coat all the ingredients evenly.
4. **Garnish and Serve:**
    - Sprinkle with chopped fresh cilantro, crumbled feta cheese (if using), and toasted seeds.
    - Serve immediately for the best texture and flavor.

Enjoy:

- Enjoy your refreshing Papaya and Avocado Salad with Lime Vinaigrette!

This salad is a vibrant, tropical dish that combines creamy avocado and sweet papaya with a tangy lime vinaigrette, making it perfect as a light lunch or a colorful side.

Caribbean Jerk Beef Tacos

Ingredients:

For the Jerk Beef:

- 1 lb ground beef
- 2 tbsp jerk seasoning (store-bought or homemade)
- 1 tbsp olive oil
- 1 small onion, finely chopped
- 2 cloves garlic, minced
- 1 red bell pepper, chopped
- 1/2 cup beef or vegetable broth
- 1 tbsp lime juice
- Salt and black pepper to taste

For the Tacos:

- 8 small corn or flour tortillas
- 1 cup shredded lettuce
- 1 cup diced tomatoes
- 1/2 cup diced red onion
- 1/4 cup fresh cilantro, chopped
- 1/2 cup crumbled feta cheese or shredded cheddar (optional)
- Lime wedges (for serving)

For the Optional Salsa (if desired):

- 1 cup diced mango
- 1/4 cup chopped red onion
- 1/4 cup chopped cilantro
- 1 tbsp lime juice
- Salt and pepper to taste

Instructions:

1. **Cook the Jerk Beef:**
   - Heat olive oil in a large skillet over medium heat.
   - Add the chopped onion and cook until translucent, about 5 minutes.
   - Stir in the garlic and cook for another minute.
   - Add the ground beef and cook until browned, breaking it up with a spoon.
   - Stir in the jerk seasoning and chopped red bell pepper.
   - Pour in the beef broth and lime juice, and simmer for 5-7 minutes until the liquid is reduced and the flavors are well combined.
   - Season with salt and black pepper to taste.
2. **Prepare the Optional Salsa (if using):**
   - In a bowl, combine diced mango, red onion, cilantro, lime juice, salt, and pepper.
   - Mix well and set aside.

3. **Warm the Tortillas:**
    - Heat tortillas in a dry skillet over medium heat or wrap them in foil and warm in a preheated oven at 350°F (175°C) for 10 minutes.
4. **Assemble the Tacos:**
    - Spoon the jerk beef mixture onto the warm tortillas.
    - Top with shredded lettuce, diced tomatoes, red onion, and cilantro.
    - Sprinkle with feta cheese or cheddar if desired.
    - Add a spoonful of the mango salsa on top if using.
5. **Serve:**
    - Serve the tacos with lime wedges on the side for extra zest.

Enjoy:

- Enjoy your flavorful Caribbean Jerk Beef Tacos!

These tacos bring a spicy and tropical twist to a classic favorite, combining the bold flavors of jerk seasoning with fresh, vibrant toppings.

Tropical Chicken Caesar Salad

Ingredients:

For the Salad:

- 2 cups cooked chicken breast, sliced or cubed (grilled or rotisserie chicken works well)
- 6 cups Romaine lettuce, chopped
- 1 cup fresh pineapple chunks (grilled or raw)
- 1/2 cup cherry tomatoes, halved
- 1/4 cup red onion, thinly sliced
- 1/4 cup shredded Parmesan cheese
- 1/4 cup sliced almonds or croutons (optional for crunch)
- Fresh cilantro or basil, chopped (for garnish)

For the Tropical Caesar Dressing:

- 1/2 cup mayonnaise
- 1/4 cup Greek yogurt or sour cream
- 2 tbsp freshly squeezed lime juice (about 1 lime)
- 1 tbsp honey
- 2 tbsp grated Parmesan cheese
- 1 garlic clove, minced
- 1 tsp Dijon mustard
- Salt and black pepper to taste

Instructions:

1. **Prepare the Tropical Caesar Dressing:**
    - In a bowl, whisk together mayonnaise, Greek yogurt (or sour cream), lime juice, honey, grated Parmesan cheese, minced garlic, and Dijon mustard.
    - Season with salt and black pepper to taste.
    - Adjust the consistency with a little water if needed, and refrigerate until ready to use.
2. **Prepare the Salad Ingredients:**
    - If using raw pineapple, grill it for a few minutes on each side until caramelized and slightly charred. Let cool before cutting into chunks.
    - In a large bowl, combine the chopped Romaine lettuce, sliced chicken, pineapple chunks, cherry tomatoes, and red onion.
3. **Toss the Salad:**
    - Drizzle the Tropical Caesar Dressing over the salad.
    - Toss gently to coat all the ingredients evenly.
4. **Serve:**
    - Top the salad with shredded Parmesan cheese, sliced almonds or croutons (if using), and a sprinkle of fresh cilantro or basil.

Enjoy:

- Enjoy your refreshing Tropical Chicken Caesar Salad!

This salad offers a tropical twist on the classic Caesar, incorporating sweet pineapple and a zesty lime dressing for a light and flavorful meal.

Coconut-Mango Shrimp Salad

Ingredients:

For the Salad:

- 1 lb large shrimp, peeled and deveined
- 1 cup shredded coconut (sweetened or unsweetened)
- 1 tbsp olive oil
- 4 cups mixed greens (e.g., arugula, spinach, or baby kale)
- 1 ripe mango, peeled and diced
- 1/2 red bell pepper, thinly sliced
- 1/4 cup red onion, thinly sliced
- 1/4 cup chopped fresh cilantro
- 1 avocado, sliced (optional)
- 1/4 cup toasted almonds or pecans (optional, for crunch)

For the Dressing:

- 1/4 cup coconut milk
- 2 tbsp lime juice (about 1 lime)
- 1 tbsp honey or agave syrup
- 1 tbsp olive oil
- 1 garlic clove, minced
- 1/2 tsp ground cumin
- Salt and black pepper to taste

Instructions:

1. **Prepare the Shrimp:**
   - Preheat your oven to 400°F (200°C) or heat a grill pan over medium-high heat.
   - Toss the shrimp with olive oil, salt, and black pepper.
   - Spread the shredded coconut on a plate. Press each shrimp into the coconut to coat, then arrange on a baking sheet or grill pan.
   - Bake for 8-10 minutes, or grill for 2-3 minutes per side, until the shrimp are cooked through and the coconut is golden brown.
2. **Prepare the Dressing:**
   - In a small bowl, whisk together coconut milk, lime juice, honey, olive oil, minced garlic, ground cumin, salt, and black pepper.
   - Adjust seasoning as needed and set aside.
3. **Assemble the Salad:**
   - In a large bowl, combine mixed greens, diced mango, red bell pepper, red onion, and chopped cilantro.

- Top with the cooked coconut-coated shrimp, avocado slices (if using), and toasted almonds or pecans (if using).
4. **Dress the Salad:**
    - Drizzle the coconut-lime dressing over the salad.
    - Toss gently to coat all the ingredients evenly.
5. **Serve:**
    - Serve immediately for the freshest flavor and texture.

Enjoy:

- Enjoy your Coconut-Mango Shrimp Salad!

This salad combines sweet and savory elements with crispy coconut shrimp and a creamy coconut-lime dressing, perfect for a tropical-inspired meal.

Island-Style Stuffed Bell Peppers

Ingredients:

For the Filling:

- 4 large bell peppers (any color)
- 1 lb ground beef or turkey
- 1 cup cooked quinoa or rice
- 1/2 cup diced pineapple (fresh or canned, drained)
- 1/2 cup black beans, rinsed and drained
- 1/2 cup corn kernels (fresh, frozen, or canned)
- 1 small red onion, finely chopped
- 2 cloves garlic, minced
- 1 tsp ground cumin
- 1/2 tsp smoked paprika
- 1/2 tsp dried oregano
- 1/4 tsp cayenne pepper (optional, for heat)
- 1/2 cup shredded cheddar or Monterey Jack cheese
- Salt and black pepper to taste

For the Topping:

- 1/4 cup shredded cheese (optional)
- Fresh cilantro or parsley, chopped (for garnish)

Instructions:

1. **Prepare the Bell Peppers:**
   - Preheat your oven to 375°F (190°C).
   - Slice the tops off the bell peppers and remove the seeds and membranes. Set aside.
2. **Cook the Filling:**
   - Heat a large skillet over medium heat and cook the ground beef or turkey until browned, breaking it up with a spoon.
   - Add the chopped onion and cook until softened, about 5 minutes.
   - Stir in the minced garlic, cumin, smoked paprika, oregano, and cayenne pepper (if using). Cook for 1-2 minutes until fragrant.
   - Add the diced pineapple, black beans, corn, and cooked quinoa or rice. Stir to combine and cook for an additional 5 minutes.
   - Season with salt and black pepper to taste.
3. **Stuff the Peppers:**
   - Spoon the filling into each bell pepper, packing it in tightly.

- Place the stuffed peppers upright in a baking dish. If desired, sprinkle additional shredded cheese on top of each pepper.
4. **Bake:**
    - Cover the baking dish with foil and bake for 25-30 minutes, or until the peppers are tender.
    - Remove the foil and bake for an additional 5-10 minutes, or until the cheese is melted and bubbly.
5. **Serve:**
    - Garnish with chopped fresh cilantro or parsley.
    - Serve warm.

Enjoy:

- Enjoy your flavorful Island-Style Stuffed Bell Peppers!

These stuffed peppers bring a tropical twist with pineapple and a mix of savory and sweet flavors, perfect for a satisfying and vibrant meal.

Grilled Pineapple and Teriyaki Chicken Sandwiches

Ingredients:

For the Chicken Marinade:

- 1/2 cup teriyaki sauce
- 2 tbsp soy sauce
- 2 tbsp honey or brown sugar
- 2 cloves garlic, minced
- 1 tbsp grated fresh ginger

For the Sandwiches:

- 4 boneless, skinless chicken breasts
- 4 slices fresh pineapple (or canned, drained)
- 4 hamburger buns or sandwich rolls
- 4 tbsp mayonnaise or aioli
- 1 cup shredded lettuce
- 1/2 red onion, thinly sliced
- 1/2 cup sliced cucumber (optional)
- 1 tbsp sesame seeds (optional, for garnish)

Instructions:

1. **Marinate the Chicken:**
   - In a bowl, combine teriyaki sauce, soy sauce, honey, minced garlic, and grated ginger.
   - Add the chicken breasts to the marinade, making sure they are well-coated. Cover and refrigerate for at least 30 minutes, or up to 2 hours for more flavor.
2. **Grill the Chicken and Pineapple:**
   - Preheat your grill to medium-high heat.
   - Remove the chicken from the marinade and grill for 6-8 minutes per side, or until fully cooked and the internal temperature reaches 165°F (74°C).
   - While the chicken is grilling, place the pineapple slices on the grill and cook for 2-3 minutes per side, until caramelized and grill marks appear.
3. **Assemble the Sandwiches:**
   - Toast the hamburger buns or sandwich rolls on the grill for about 1 minute, or until lightly golden.
   - Spread mayonnaise or aioli on the bottom half of each bun.
   - Place a grilled chicken breast on each bun, followed by a grilled pineapple slice.
   - Top with shredded lettuce, sliced red onion, and cucumber slices (if using).
   - Sprinkle with sesame seeds if desired.
   - Close the sandwiches with the top half of the bun.
4. **Serve:**
   - Serve the sandwiches warm.

Enjoy:

- Enjoy your delicious Grilled Pineapple and Teriyaki Chicken Sandwiches!

These sandwiches offer a sweet and savory combination with juicy grilled chicken, caramelized pineapple, and a tangy teriyaki sauce, perfect for a flavorful meal.

Caribbean Fish and Chips

Ingredients:

For the Fish:

- 1 lb white fish fillets (such as cod, snapper, or tilapia)
- 1 cup all-purpose flour
- 1 tsp paprika
- 1/2 tsp garlic powder
- 1/2 tsp onion powder
- 1/2 tsp cayenne pepper (optional, for heat)
- Salt and black pepper to taste
- 1 cup buttermilk
- 1 cup panko breadcrumbs
- 1/2 cup shredded coconut (optional, for extra flavor)
- Vegetable oil, for frying

For the Chips:

- 4 large russet potatoes, peeled and cut into thick fries
- 2 tbsp vegetable oil
- Salt and black pepper to taste
- 1 tsp paprika
- 1/2 tsp garlic powder

For the Caribbean Tartare Sauce:

- 1/2 cup mayonnaise
- 2 tbsp chopped pickles or relish
- 1 tbsp capers, chopped
- 1 tbsp lime juice
- 1 tbsp chopped fresh cilantro
- 1/2 tsp jerk seasoning (adjust to taste)
- Salt and black pepper to taste

Instructions:

1. **Prepare the Chips:**
    - Preheat your oven to 425°F (220°C).
    - Toss the potato fries with vegetable oil, salt, black pepper, paprika, and garlic powder.
    - Spread the fries in a single layer on a baking sheet.
    - Bake for 25-30 minutes, flipping halfway through, until crispy and golden brown.

2. **Prepare the Fish:**
   - In a bowl, combine flour, paprika, garlic powder, onion powder, cayenne pepper, salt, and black pepper.
   - Place the buttermilk in another bowl.
   - In a third bowl, combine panko breadcrumbs and shredded coconut (if using).
   - Dip each fish fillet into the flour mixture, then into the buttermilk, and finally coat with the panko-coconut mixture.
3. **Fry the Fish:**
   - Heat vegetable oil in a large skillet or deep fryer over medium-high heat to 350°F (175°C).
   - Fry the fish fillets in batches for 3-4 minutes per side, or until golden brown and crispy. Avoid overcrowding the pan.
   - Remove the fish with a slotted spoon and drain on paper towels.
4. **Prepare the Caribbean Tartare Sauce:**
   - In a bowl, mix together mayonnaise, pickles or relish, capers, lime juice, chopped cilantro, and jerk seasoning.
   - Season with salt and black pepper to taste.
5. **Serve:**
   - Serve the crispy fish with the baked chips and a side of Caribbean tartare sauce.
   - Garnish with additional lime wedges and fresh cilantro if desired.

Enjoy:

- Enjoy your flavorful Caribbean Fish and Chips!

This dish combines crispy fish with seasoned fries and a tangy Caribbean-inspired tartare sauce, offering a delightful twist on a classic favorite.

Pineapple-Jalapeño Chicken Wraps

Ingredients:

For the Chicken Marinade:

- 1 lb boneless, skinless chicken breasts or thighs
- 1/4 cup pineapple juice
- 2 tbsp soy sauce
- 1 tbsp honey
- 1 tbsp lime juice
- 1 clove garlic, minced
- 1 tsp ground ginger
- 1 jalapeño pepper, seeded and finely chopped (adjust to taste)
- Salt and black pepper to taste

For the Wraps:

- 4 large flour or whole wheat tortillas
- 1 cup shredded lettuce
- 1 cup diced fresh pineapple
- 1/2 red bell pepper, thinly sliced
- 1/4 cup red onion, thinly sliced
- 1 avocado, sliced
- 1/2 cup shredded cheese (cheddar, Monterey Jack, or your choice)
- Fresh cilantro or mint leaves (for garnish)

For the Pineapple-Jalapeño Sauce:

- 1/2 cup mayonnaise
- 2 tbsp pineapple juice
- 1 tbsp lime juice
- 1 jalapeño pepper, seeded and minced
- 1 tbsp honey
- Salt and black pepper to taste

Instructions:

1. **Marinate the Chicken:**
   - In a bowl, combine pineapple juice, soy sauce, honey, lime juice, minced garlic, ground ginger, and chopped jalapeño.
   - Season with salt and black pepper.
   - Add the chicken breasts or thighs and marinate in the refrigerator for at least 30 minutes, or up to 2 hours for more flavor.

2. **Cook the Chicken:**
   - Preheat a grill or skillet over medium-high heat.
   - Remove the chicken from the marinade and cook for 6-8 minutes per side, or until the internal temperature reaches 165°F (74°C) and the chicken is cooked through.
   - Let the chicken rest for a few minutes before slicing into strips.
3. **Prepare the Pineapple-Jalapeño Sauce:**
   - In a small bowl, mix together mayonnaise, pineapple juice, lime juice, minced jalapeño, and honey.
   - Season with salt and black pepper to taste. Adjust the heat level by adding more or less jalapeño.
4. **Assemble the Wraps:**
   - Warm the tortillas in a dry skillet or microwave.
   - Spread a generous amount of the pineapple-jalapeño sauce on each tortilla.
   - Top with shredded lettuce, diced pineapple, sliced red bell pepper, red onion, avocado slices, and shredded cheese.
   - Place the sliced chicken on top.
5. **Wrap and Serve:**
   - Roll up each tortilla tightly to enclose the filling.
   - Slice in half diagonally, if desired, and garnish with fresh cilantro or mint leaves.

Enjoy:

- Enjoy your delicious Pineapple-Jalapeño Chicken Wraps!

These wraps combine sweet and spicy flavors with tender chicken, fresh vegetables, and a creamy pineapple-jalapeño sauce for a refreshing and satisfying meal.

Tropical Shrimp and Avocado Salad

Ingredients:

For the Salad:

- 1 lb large shrimp, peeled and deveined
- 2 tbsp olive oil
- 1 tsp paprika
- 1/2 tsp garlic powder
- 1/2 tsp ground cumin
- Salt and black pepper to taste
- 4 cups mixed greens (e.g., spinach, arugula, or baby kale)
- 1 ripe avocado, diced
- 1 cup diced fresh mango
- 1/2 cup cherry tomatoes, halved
- 1/4 cup red onion, thinly sliced
- 1/4 cup chopped fresh cilantro
- 1/4 cup chopped toasted almonds or pecans (optional, for crunch)

For the Citrus Vinaigrette:

- 1/4 cup fresh orange juice (about 1 orange)
- 2 tbsp fresh lime juice (about 1 lime)
- 2 tbsp olive oil
- 1 tbsp honey or agave syrup
- 1 garlic clove, minced
- 1/2 tsp ground cumin
- Salt and black pepper to taste

Instructions:

1. **Cook the Shrimp:**
   - Preheat a grill or skillet over medium-high heat.
   - In a bowl, toss the shrimp with olive oil, paprika, garlic powder, ground cumin, salt, and black pepper.
   - Grill or sauté the shrimp for 2-3 minutes per side, or until pink and opaque. Remove from heat and set aside to cool slightly.
2. **Prepare the Citrus Vinaigrette:**
   - In a small bowl, whisk together orange juice, lime juice, olive oil, honey, minced garlic, ground cumin, salt, and black pepper.
   - Adjust seasoning to taste and set aside.
3. **Assemble the Salad:**

        - In a large bowl, combine mixed greens, diced avocado, diced mango, cherry tomatoes, red onion, and chopped cilantro.
        - Add the cooked shrimp on top.
4. **Dress the Salad:**
        - Drizzle the citrus vinaigrette over the salad.
        - Toss gently to coat all ingredients evenly.
5. **Serve:**
        - Garnish with toasted almonds or pecans if desired.
        - Serve immediately for the freshest flavor.

Enjoy:

- Enjoy your vibrant and refreshing Tropical Shrimp and Avocado Salad!

This salad features a delightful mix of tropical fruits, creamy avocado, and zesty shrimp, all topped with a tangy citrus vinaigrette for a perfect light meal.

Coconut-Basil Chicken Bites

Ingredients:

For the Chicken Bites:

- 1 lb boneless, skinless chicken breasts or thighs, cut into bite-sized pieces
- 1/2 cup all-purpose flour
- 1/2 tsp paprika
- 1/2 tsp garlic powder
- 1/2 tsp onion powder
- Salt and black pepper to taste
- 2 large eggs
- 1 cup shredded coconut (sweetened or unsweetened)
- 1/2 cup panko breadcrumbs
- Vegetable oil, for frying

For the Basil Dipping Sauce:

- 1/2 cup mayonnaise
- 2 tbsp chopped fresh basil
- 1 tbsp lime juice
- 1 tsp honey
- 1 garlic clove, minced
- Salt and black pepper to taste

Instructions:

1. **Prepare the Chicken Bites:**
    - In a shallow bowl, combine flour, paprika, garlic powder, onion powder, salt, and black pepper.
    - In another bowl, beat the eggs.
    - In a third bowl, mix shredded coconut and panko breadcrumbs.
    - Dredge each chicken piece in the flour mixture, then dip into the beaten eggs, and finally coat with the coconut-panko mixture.
2. **Fry the Chicken Bites:**
    - Heat vegetable oil in a large skillet over medium-high heat.
    - Fry the chicken bites in batches for 3-4 minutes per side, or until golden brown and cooked through (internal temperature should reach 165°F or 74°C). Avoid overcrowding the pan.
    - Remove the chicken bites with a slotted spoon and drain on paper towels.
3. **Prepare the Basil Dipping Sauce:**
    - In a small bowl, mix together mayonnaise, chopped fresh basil, lime juice, honey, and minced garlic.

- - Season with salt and black pepper to taste. Adjust the flavors as needed.
4. **Serve:**
    - Arrange the coconut-basil chicken bites on a serving platter.
    - Serve with the basil dipping sauce on the side.

Enjoy:

- Enjoy your crispy and flavorful Coconut-Basil Chicken Bites!

These chicken bites are coated in a crunchy coconut and panko mixture, paired with a tangy and creamy basil dipping sauce for a delightful appetizer or snack.

Island-Style Turkey Burgers

Ingredients:

For the Turkey Burgers:

- 1 lb ground turkey
- 1/4 cup finely chopped fresh pineapple
- 1/4 cup finely chopped red bell pepper
- 2 green onions, finely chopped
- 2 cloves garlic, minced
- 1 tbsp soy sauce
- 1 tbsp grated fresh ginger
- 1 tsp ground cumin
- 1/2 tsp paprika
- 1/4 tsp cayenne pepper (optional, for heat)
- Salt and black pepper to taste
- 4 hamburger buns

For the Tropical Topping:

- 1 ripe avocado, sliced
- 1/2 cup pineapple salsa (store-bought or homemade)
- 1 cup shredded lettuce
- 1 tomato, sliced

For the Pineapple Salsa (Optional):

- 1 cup diced fresh pineapple
- 1/2 cup diced red onion
- 1/4 cup chopped fresh cilantro
- 1 jalapeño pepper, seeded and minced (optional, for heat)
- 1 tbsp lime juice
- Salt and black pepper to taste

Instructions:

1. **Prepare the Pineapple Salsa (Optional):**
   - In a bowl, combine diced pineapple, diced red onion, chopped cilantro, minced jalapeño (if using), and lime juice.
   - Season with salt and black pepper to taste. Mix well and set aside.
2. **Prepare the Turkey Burgers:**

- In a large bowl, combine ground turkey, chopped pineapple, red bell pepper, green onions, minced garlic, soy sauce, grated ginger, ground cumin, paprika, cayenne pepper (if using), salt, and black pepper.
- Mix gently until all ingredients are well combined. Be careful not to overmix.
- Divide the mixture into 4 equal portions and shape each portion into a patty.

3. **Cook the Turkey Burgers:**
   - Preheat a grill or skillet over medium-high heat.
   - Cook the turkey burgers for 5-6 minutes per side, or until they reach an internal temperature of 165°F (74°C) and are cooked through.
   - If grilling, you can toast the hamburger buns on the grill for about 1 minute, or until lightly golden.

4. **Assemble the Burgers:**
   - Spread a layer of pineapple salsa on the bottom half of each toasted bun.
   - Place a cooked turkey burger on top of the salsa.
   - Top with sliced avocado, shredded lettuce, and tomato slices.
   - Spread additional pineapple salsa on the top half of the bun, if desired.
   - Close the burgers with the top bun.

5. **Serve:**
   - Serve the island-style turkey burgers immediately, with additional pineapple salsa on the side if desired.

Enjoy:

- Enjoy your flavorful and tropical Island-Style Turkey Burgers!

These turkey burgers are infused with island flavors and topped with fresh, tropical ingredients for a delicious and unique twist on a classic burger.

Mango-Coconut Chicken Stir-Fry

Ingredients:

For the Turkey Burgers:

- 1 lb ground turkey
- 1/4 cup finely chopped fresh pineapple
- 1/4 cup finely chopped red bell pepper
- 2 green onions, finely chopped
- 2 cloves garlic, minced
- 1 tbsp soy sauce
- 1 tbsp grated fresh ginger
- 1 tsp ground cumin
- 1/2 tsp paprika
- 1/4 tsp cayenne pepper (optional, for heat)
- Salt and black pepper to taste
- 4 hamburger buns

For the Tropical Topping:

- 1 ripe avocado, sliced
- 1/2 cup pineapple salsa (store-bought or homemade)
- 1 cup shredded lettuce
- 1 tomato, sliced

For the Pineapple Salsa (Optional):

- 1 cup diced fresh pineapple
- 1/2 cup diced red onion
- 1/4 cup chopped fresh cilantro
- 1 jalapeño pepper, seeded and minced (optional, for heat)
- 1 tbsp lime juice
- Salt and black pepper to taste

Instructions:

1. **Prepare the Pineapple Salsa (Optional):**
   - In a bowl, combine diced pineapple, diced red onion, chopped cilantro, minced jalapeño (if using), and lime juice.
   - Season with salt and black pepper to taste. Mix well and set aside.
2. **Prepare the Turkey Burgers:**

- In a large bowl, combine ground turkey, chopped pineapple, red bell pepper, green onions, minced garlic, soy sauce, grated ginger, ground cumin, paprika, cayenne pepper (if using), salt, and black pepper.
- Mix gently until all ingredients are well combined. Be careful not to overmix.
- Divide the mixture into 4 equal portions and shape each portion into a patty.

3. **Cook the Turkey Burgers:**
    - Preheat a grill or skillet over medium-high heat.
    - Cook the turkey burgers for 5-6 minutes per side, or until they reach an internal temperature of 165°F (74°C) and are cooked through.
    - If grilling, you can toast the hamburger buns on the grill for about 1 minute, or until lightly golden.
4. **Assemble the Burgers:**
    - Spread a layer of pineapple salsa on the bottom half of each toasted bun.
    - Place a cooked turkey burger on top of the salsa.
    - Top with sliced avocado, shredded lettuce, and tomato slices.
    - Spread additional pineapple salsa on the top half of the bun, if desired.
    - Close the burgers with the top bun.
5. **Serve:**
    - Serve the island-style turkey burgers immediately, with additional pineapple salsa on the side if desired.

Enjoy:

- Enjoy your flavorful and tropical Island-Style Turkey Burgers!

These turkey burgers are infused with island flavors and topped with fresh, tropical ingredients for a delicious and unique twist on a classic burger.

Pineapple-Glazed Chicken Skewers

Ingredients:

For the Chicken Marinade:

- 1 lb boneless, skinless chicken breasts or thighs, cut into bite-sized pieces
- 1/4 cup soy sauce
- 2 tbsp pineapple juice
- 2 tbsp honey
- 1 tbsp lime juice
- 2 cloves garlic, minced
- 1 tbsp grated fresh ginger
- 1/2 tsp ground cumin
- Salt and black pepper to taste

For the Pineapple Glaze:

- 1/2 cup pineapple juice
- 1/4 cup soy sauce
- 2 tbsp honey
- 1 tbsp cornstarch mixed with 1 tbsp water (slurry)
- 1 clove garlic, minced
- 1 tsp grated fresh ginger

For Assembly:

- 1 bell pepper, cut into chunks
- 1 red onion, cut into chunks
- 1 cup fresh pineapple chunks
- Wooden or metal skewers (soaked in water if wooden)

Instructions:

1. **Marinate the Chicken:**
   - In a bowl, combine soy sauce, pineapple juice, honey, lime juice, minced garlic, grated ginger, ground cumin, salt, and black pepper.
   - Add the chicken pieces and toss to coat. Cover and refrigerate for at least 30 minutes or up to 2 hours.
2. **Prepare the Pineapple Glaze:**
   - In a small saucepan, combine pineapple juice, soy sauce, honey, minced garlic, and grated ginger.
   - Bring to a simmer over medium heat.

- Stir in the cornstarch slurry and continue to cook, stirring constantly, until the glaze thickens. Remove from heat and set aside.

3. **Assemble the Skewers:**
   - Preheat your grill or grill pan to medium-high heat.
   - Thread the marinated chicken pieces onto the skewers, alternating with bell pepper chunks, red onion chunks, and pineapple chunks.

4. **Grill the Skewers:**
   - Grill the skewers for 8-10 minutes, turning occasionally, until the chicken is cooked through and has an internal temperature of 165°F (74°C). Baste with the pineapple glaze during the last few minutes of grilling.

5. **Serve:**
   - Brush the skewers with additional pineapple glaze before serving.
   - Serve warm with extra pineapple glaze on the side for dipping.

Enjoy:

- Enjoy your sweet and savory Pineapple-Glazed Chicken Skewers!

These skewers are packed with tropical flavors and offer a perfect balance of sweetness from the pineapple and savory notes from the chicken and glaze.

Caribbean-Style Veggie Burger

Ingredients:

For the Veggie Burger Patties:

- 1 can (15 oz) black beans, drained and rinsed
- 1/2 cup cooked quinoa or brown rice
- 1/2 cup finely chopped red bell pepper
- 1/4 cup finely chopped red onion
- 1/2 cup grated carrots
- 2 cloves garlic, minced
- 1 tbsp fresh cilantro, chopped
- 1 tsp ground cumin
- 1/2 tsp paprika
- 1/4 tsp cayenne pepper (optional, for heat)
- 1/4 cup breadcrumbs or oat flour (for binding)
- 1 egg (or 1 flax egg for a vegan option)
- Salt and black pepper to taste

For the Caribbean Sauce:

- 1/4 cup mayonnaise
- 1 tbsp jerk seasoning
- 1 tbsp lime juice
- 1 tsp honey or agave syrup
- 1 clove garlic, minced

For Serving:

- 4 whole wheat or regular hamburger buns
- 1 avocado, sliced
- 1 tomato, sliced
- 1 cup shredded lettuce
- 1/2 cup pineapple salsa (store-bought or homemade)

For the Pineapple Salsa (Optional):

- 1 cup diced fresh pineapple
- 1/2 cup diced red onion
- 1/4 cup chopped fresh cilantro
- 1 jalapeño pepper, seeded and minced (optional, for heat)
- 1 tbsp lime juice
- Salt and black pepper to taste

Instructions:

1. **Prepare the Pineapple Salsa (Optional):**
    - In a bowl, combine diced pineapple, diced red onion, chopped cilantro, minced jalapeño (if using), and lime juice.
    - Season with salt and black pepper to taste. Mix well and set aside.
2. **Prepare the Veggie Burger Patties:**
    - In a large bowl, mash the black beans with a fork or potato masher until mostly smooth but still a bit chunky.
    - Add cooked quinoa or rice, chopped red bell pepper, red onion, grated carrots, minced garlic, chopped cilantro, ground cumin, paprika, cayenne pepper (if using), breadcrumbs or oat flour, and egg (or flax egg).
    - Mix until well combined. Season with salt and black pepper.
    - Form the mixture into 4 patties.
3. **Cook the Veggie Burger Patties:**
    - Preheat a grill or skillet over medium heat and lightly grease with oil.
    - Cook the patties for 5-6 minutes per side, or until they are browned and heated through.
4. **Prepare the Caribbean Sauce:**
    - In a small bowl, mix together mayonnaise, jerk seasoning, lime juice, honey or agave syrup, and minced garlic.
    - Stir until well combined.
5. **Assemble the Burgers:**
    - Toast the hamburger buns if desired.
    - Spread a layer of Caribbean sauce on the bottom half of each bun.
    - Place a veggie burger patty on top of the sauce.
    - Add sliced avocado, tomato slices, shredded lettuce, and a spoonful of pineapple salsa (if using).
    - Top with the other half of the bun.
6. **Serve:**
    - Serve the Caribbean-style veggie burgers immediately.

Enjoy:

- Enjoy your vibrant and flavorful Caribbean-Style Veggie Burgers!

These veggie burgers are packed with tropical flavors and textures, offering a delicious and hearty alternative to traditional burgers.

Tropical BBQ Chicken Salad

Ingredients:

For the Salad:

- 2 cups cooked chicken, shredded or diced (grilled or rotisserie)
- 4 cups mixed greens (e.g., romaine, spinach, or arugula)
- 1 cup fresh pineapple chunks
- 1/2 cup cherry tomatoes, halved
- 1/4 cup red onion, thinly sliced
- 1/2 cup sliced cucumber
- 1 avocado, sliced
- 1/4 cup crumbled feta cheese or shredded cheddar cheese
- 1/4 cup chopped fresh cilantro

For the BBQ Dressing:

- 1/4 cup BBQ sauce (use your favorite brand or homemade)
- 2 tbsp plain Greek yogurt or mayonnaise
- 1 tbsp lime juice
- 1 tbsp honey
- 1 clove garlic, minced
- Salt and black pepper to taste

Instructions:

1. **Prepare the BBQ Dressing:**
   - In a small bowl, whisk together BBQ sauce, Greek yogurt or mayonnaise, lime juice, honey, and minced garlic.
   - Season with salt and black pepper to taste. Adjust sweetness or tanginess if needed.
2. **Assemble the Salad:**
   - In a large bowl, combine mixed greens, fresh pineapple chunks, cherry tomatoes, red onion, sliced cucumber, and avocado.
   - Top with shredded or diced chicken.
3. **Add the Cheese and Cilantro:**
   - Sprinkle crumbled feta cheese or shredded cheddar cheese over the top.
   - Garnish with chopped fresh cilantro.
4. **Serve:**
   - Drizzle the BBQ dressing over the salad or serve it on the side.
   - Toss gently to combine, if desired, or leave the salad layered.

Enjoy:

- Enjoy your refreshing and flavorful Tropical BBQ Chicken Salad!

This salad combines tropical sweetness with savory BBQ flavors for a satisfying and unique meal.

Coconut and Pineapple Chicken Curry

Ingredients:

For the Curry:

- 1 lb boneless, skinless chicken thighs or breasts, cut into bite-sized pieces
- 1 tbsp vegetable oil
- 1 medium onion, finely chopped
- 2 cloves garlic, minced
- 1 tbsp fresh ginger, grated
- 2 tbsp curry powder
- 1 tsp ground turmeric
- 1/2 tsp ground cumin
- 1/4 tsp red chili flakes (optional, for heat)
- 1 cup coconut milk
- 1 cup fresh pineapple chunks
- 1 cup diced tomatoes (canned or fresh)
- 1 tbsp soy sauce or tamari
- Salt and black pepper to taste
- Fresh cilantro, chopped (for garnish)
- Cooked rice or naan (for serving)

Instructions:

1. **Cook the Chicken:**
    - Heat vegetable oil in a large skillet or saucepan over medium heat.
    - Add chopped onion and cook until soft and translucent, about 5 minutes.
    - Stir in minced garlic and grated ginger, and cook for another minute.
2. **Add Spices:**
    - Add curry powder, ground turmeric, ground cumin, and red chili flakes (if using). Cook for 1-2 minutes until fragrant.
3. **Simmer the Curry:**
    - Add the chicken pieces to the skillet, stirring to coat them with the spices.
    - Pour in the coconut milk, diced tomatoes, and soy sauce. Stir well.
    - Bring to a simmer, reduce heat to low, and cook for 15-20 minutes, or until the chicken is cooked through and tender.
4. **Add Pineapple:**
    - Stir in the pineapple chunks and cook for an additional 5 minutes, allowing the flavors to meld and the pineapple to warm through.
5. **Season and Serve:**
    - Season with salt and black pepper to taste.
    - Garnish with chopped fresh cilantro.

6. **Serve:**
    - Serve the curry over cooked rice or with naan bread.

Enjoy:

- Enjoy your tropical and flavorful Coconut and Pineapple Chicken Curry!

This dish blends the sweetness of pineapple with the creamy richness of coconut milk and aromatic spices for a delightful and comforting meal.

Island-Style Beef and Vegetable Stir-Fry

Ingredients:

- 1 lb beef sirloin, thinly sliced
- 2 tbsp vegetable oil
- 1 red bell pepper, sliced
- 1 green bell pepper, sliced
- 1 cup snap peas
- 1 cup carrots, sliced
- 1 onion, sliced
- 3 cloves garlic, minced
- 1 tbsp fresh ginger, minced
- 1/4 cup soy sauce
- 2 tbsp pineapple juice
- 1 tbsp brown sugar
- 1 tbsp cornstarch mixed with 2 tbsp water
- Cooked rice or noodles (for serving)
- Fresh cilantro or green onions for garnish (optional)

Instructions:

1. Heat oil in a large pan over medium-high heat.
2. Add beef and stir-fry until browned. Remove and set aside.
3. In the same pan, add onion, garlic, and ginger; cook until fragrant.
4. Add peppers, snap peas, and carrots; stir-fry until tender-crisp.
5. Return beef to the pan.
6. Mix soy sauce, pineapple juice, and brown sugar. Pour over beef and vegetables.
7. Add cornstarch mixture and cook until sauce thickens.
8. Serve over rice or noodles. Garnish with cilantro or green onions if desired.

Tropical Tuna Salad with Mango

Ingredients:

- 1 can (5 oz) tuna, drained
- 1 ripe mango, peeled and diced
- 1/2 cup red bell pepper, finely diced
- 1/4 cup red onion, finely diced
- 1/4 cup celery, finely chopped
- 2 tbsp fresh cilantro, chopped
- 2 tbsp lime juice
- 2 tbsp extra-virgin olive oil
- 1 tsp honey
- Salt and pepper to taste
- 4 cups mixed greens or lettuce (for serving)

Instructions:

1. In a large bowl, combine the tuna, mango, red bell pepper, red onion, celery, and cilantro.
2. In a small bowl, whisk together lime juice, olive oil, honey, salt, and pepper.
3. Pour the dressing over the tuna mixture and toss gently to combine.
4. Serve the salad over a bed of mixed greens or lettuce.

Enjoy your tropical twist on a classic tuna salad!

Grilled Coconut-Lime Chicken

Ingredients:

- 4 boneless, skinless chicken breasts
- 1 cup coconut milk
- Zest and juice of 2 limes
- 3 cloves garlic, minced
- 1 tbsp fresh ginger, minced
- 2 tbsp soy sauce
- 1 tbsp honey
- 1/2 tsp ground cumin
- 1/2 tsp paprika
- Salt and pepper to taste
- Fresh cilantro for garnish (optional)
- Lime wedges for serving (optional)

Instructions:

1. **Marinate the Chicken:** In a bowl, combine coconut milk, lime zest, lime juice, garlic, ginger, soy sauce, honey, cumin, paprika, salt, and pepper. Mix well.
2. Add chicken breasts to the marinade, making sure they are fully coated. Cover and refrigerate for at least 1 hour, or up to 4 hours for more flavor.
3. **Preheat the Grill:** Heat your grill to medium-high heat.
4. **Grill the Chicken:** Remove chicken from the marinade and discard the marinade. Grill chicken for 6-7 minutes per side, or until fully cooked and the internal temperature reaches 165°F (74°C).
5. **Serve:** Garnish with fresh cilantro and lime wedges if desired.

Enjoy your flavorful and tropical grilled chicken!

Jerk-Spiced Pulled Pork Tacos

Ingredients:

For the Pulled Pork:

- 3-4 lbs pork shoulder or butt
- 2 tbsp jerk seasoning (store-bought or homemade, see below)
- 1 tbsp olive oil
- 1 onion, chopped
- 4 cloves garlic, minced
- 1 cup chicken broth
- 1/2 cup orange juice
- 2 tbsp soy sauce
- 2 tbsp brown sugar
- 1 tbsp apple cider vinegar
- 1-2 Scotch bonnet peppers, seeded and finely chopped (optional, for extra heat)

For the Jerk Seasoning (if making your own):

- 1 tbsp allspice
- 1 tbsp thyme
- 1 tsp cinnamon
- 1 tsp nutmeg
- 1 tsp paprika
- 1 tsp cayenne pepper
- 1 tsp garlic powder
- 1 tsp onion powder
- Salt and pepper to taste

For the Tacos:

- Small tortillas (flour or corn)
- Shredded cabbage or lettuce
- Sliced avocado
- Fresh cilantro, chopped
- Lime wedges
- Your favorite salsa or hot sauce

Instructions:

1. **Prepare the Jerk Seasoning:** If making your own, mix all the jerk seasoning ingredients in a small bowl. Rub the seasoning all over the pork shoulder.

2. **Cook the Pork:** Heat olive oil in a large skillet or Dutch oven over medium-high heat. Sear the pork shoulder on all sides until browned. Remove from the skillet and set aside.
3. **Sauté Aromatics:** In the same skillet, add chopped onion and garlic. Cook until softened, about 2-3 minutes.
4. **Add Liquid Ingredients:** Pour in chicken broth, orange juice, soy sauce, brown sugar, apple cider vinegar, and Scotch bonnet peppers (if using). Stir to combine.
5. **Braise the Pork:** Return the seared pork shoulder to the skillet. Bring the mixture to a boil, then reduce the heat to low. Cover and simmer for 4-5 hours, or until the pork is tender and easily shredded.
6. **Shred the Pork:** Remove the pork from the skillet and shred it using two forks. Return the shredded pork to the skillet and stir to combine with the juices. Cook for an additional 10-15 minutes, allowing the flavors to meld.
7. **Assemble the Tacos:** Warm the tortillas. Fill each tortilla with jerk-spiced pulled pork and top with shredded cabbage or lettuce, sliced avocado, fresh cilantro, and a squeeze of lime juice. Add salsa or hot sauce if desired.

Enjoy your spicy and delicious pulled pork tacos!

Pineapple and Avocado Chicken Wraps

Ingredients:

- 2 cups cooked chicken, shredded or diced (grilled, rotisserie, or poached)
- 1 ripe avocado, diced
- 1 cup fresh pineapple, diced (or use canned pineapple, drained)
- 1/4 cup red onion, finely chopped
- 1/4 cup fresh cilantro, chopped
- 2 tbsp lime juice
- 1 tbsp honey
- Salt and pepper to taste
- 4 large tortillas (flour or whole wheat)
- 1 cup shredded lettuce or mixed greens

Instructions:

1. **Prepare the Dressing:** In a small bowl, whisk together lime juice, honey, salt, and pepper. Adjust seasoning to taste.
2. **Mix the Filling:** In a large bowl, combine the shredded chicken, diced avocado, diced pineapple, chopped red onion, and fresh cilantro. Gently toss with the lime-honey dressing until well mixed.
3. **Assemble the Wraps:** Lay out the tortillas on a flat surface. Place a handful of shredded lettuce or mixed greens in the center of each tortilla.
4. **Add the Filling:** Spoon the chicken, pineapple, and avocado mixture on top of the greens.
5. **Wrap It Up:** Fold in the sides of the tortilla, then roll it up from the bottom to enclose the filling.
6. **Serve:** Cut the wraps in half if desired, and serve immediately.

Enjoy these vibrant and refreshing wraps!

Coconut-Curry Beef Stew

Ingredients:

- 2 lbs beef stew meat, cubed
- 2 tbsp vegetable oil
- 1 large onion, chopped
- 3 cloves garlic, minced
- 1 tbsp fresh ginger, minced
- 2 tbsp curry powder
- 1 tsp ground turmeric
- 1/2 tsp cayenne pepper (optional, for heat)
- 1 can (14 oz) coconut milk
- 2 cups beef broth
- 2 large carrots, sliced
- 2 potatoes, peeled and cubed
- 1 red bell pepper, chopped
- 1 cup frozen peas
- Salt and pepper to taste
- Fresh cilantro for garnish (optional)

Instructions:

1. **Brown the Beef:** Heat oil in a large pot or Dutch oven over medium-high heat. Add beef cubes and brown on all sides. Remove and set aside.
2. **Sauté Aromatics:** In the same pot, add onion, garlic, and ginger. Cook until softened, about 5 minutes.
3. **Add Spices:** Stir in curry powder, turmeric, and cayenne pepper. Cook for 1 minute until fragrant.
4. **Simmer the Stew:** Return the beef to the pot. Add coconut milk and beef broth. Bring to a simmer, then reduce heat and cover. Cook for 1.5 hours, or until beef is tender.
5. **Add Vegetables:** Add carrots, potatoes, and bell pepper. Simmer for another 30 minutes, until vegetables are tender.
6. **Finish:** Stir in frozen peas and cook for an additional 5 minutes. Season with salt and pepper to taste.
7. **Serve:** Garnish with fresh cilantro if desired and serve hot.

Enjoy your rich and flavorful beef stew!

Tropical Fruit and Chicken Wraps

Ingredients:

- 2 cups cooked chicken, shredded or diced
- 1 cup pineapple, diced
- 1 cup mango, diced
- 1/2 cup red bell pepper, thinly sliced
- 1/4 cup red onion, finely chopped
- 1/4 cup fresh cilantro, chopped
- 2 tbsp lime juice
- 2 tbsp honey
- Salt and pepper to taste
- 4 large tortillas (flour or whole wheat)
- 1 cup mixed greens or shredded lettuce

Instructions:

1. **Prepare the Dressing:** In a small bowl, whisk together lime juice, honey, salt, and pepper.
2. **Mix the Filling:** In a large bowl, combine chicken, pineapple, mango, red bell pepper, red onion, and cilantro. Pour the lime-honey dressing over the mixture and toss gently to combine.
3. **Assemble the Wraps:** Lay out the tortillas on a flat surface. Place a handful of mixed greens or shredded lettuce in the center of each tortilla.
4. **Add the Filling:** Spoon the tropical chicken mixture on top of the greens.
5. **Wrap It Up:** Fold in the sides of the tortilla, then roll it up from the bottom to enclose the filling.
6. **Serve:** Cut the wraps in half if desired, and serve immediately.

Enjoy these vibrant and refreshing wraps!

Jamaican Jerk Chicken Salad

Ingredients:

- 2 cups cooked chicken, shredded or diced (grilled jerk chicken is ideal)
- 4 cups mixed greens or lettuce
- 1 cup cherry tomatoes, halved
- 1/2 cucumber, sliced
- 1/4 red onion, thinly sliced
- 1/2 cup mango, diced
- 1/4 cup fresh cilantro, chopped

For the Jerk Marinade/Dressing:

- 2 tbsp jerk seasoning (store-bought or homemade)
- 3 tbsp olive oil
- 2 tbsp lime juice
- 1 tbsp honey
- 1 tbsp soy sauce
- 1 garlic clove, minced
- Salt and pepper to taste

Instructions:

1. **Prepare the Dressing:** In a small bowl, whisk together jerk seasoning, olive oil, lime juice, honey, soy sauce, garlic, salt, and pepper.
2. **Assemble the Salad:** In a large bowl, combine mixed greens, cherry tomatoes, cucumber, red onion, mango, and cilantro.
3. **Add Chicken:** Toss the chicken with a little of the jerk dressing.
4. **Dress the Salad:** Drizzle the remaining jerk dressing over the salad and toss gently to combine.
5. **Serve:** Divide the salad among plates and top with jerk chicken.

Enjoy this vibrant and spicy salad!

Caribbean Pork and Pineapple Skewers

Ingredients:

- 1 lb pork tenderloin, cut into 1-inch cubes
- 1 cup fresh pineapple, cut into 1-inch chunks
- 1 red bell pepper, cut into 1-inch pieces
- 1 green bell pepper, cut into 1-inch pieces
- 1 small red onion, cut into chunks

For the Marinade:

- 1/4 cup soy sauce
- 2 tbsp brown sugar
- 2 tbsp pineapple juice
- 2 tbsp olive oil
- 1 tbsp fresh ginger, minced
- 3 cloves garlic, minced
- 1 tsp allspice
- 1/2 tsp ground cinnamon
- 1/4 tsp cayenne pepper (optional, for heat)
- Salt and pepper to taste

Instructions:

1. **Prepare the Marinade:** In a bowl, whisk together soy sauce, brown sugar, pineapple juice, olive oil, ginger, garlic, allspice, cinnamon, cayenne pepper, salt, and pepper.
2. **Marinate the Pork:** Place pork cubes in a resealable plastic bag or bowl. Pour half of the marinade over the pork, toss to coat, and refrigerate for at least 1 hour. Reserve the remaining marinade for basting.
3. **Assemble the Skewers:** Thread pork, pineapple chunks, bell peppers, and red onion onto skewers, alternating as you go.
4. **Grill the Skewers:** Preheat the grill to medium-high heat. Grill the skewers for 10-12 minutes, turning occasionally and basting with the reserved marinade, until the pork is cooked through and has a nice char.
5. **Serve:** Remove from the grill and serve hot.

Enjoy these flavorful and tropical skewers!

Spicy Pineapple Shrimp Tacos

Ingredients:

- 1 lb large shrimp, peeled and deveined
- 1 cup fresh pineapple, diced
- 2 tbsp olive oil
- 2 tbsp lime juice
- 1 tbsp honey
- 1 tsp chili powder
- 1/2 tsp cayenne pepper (adjust to taste)
- 1/2 tsp garlic powder
- Salt and pepper to taste
- 8 small tortillas (flour or corn)

For the Slaw:

- 2 cups shredded cabbage or coleslaw mix
- 1/4 cup fresh cilantro, chopped
- 2 tbsp lime juice
- 1 tbsp honey
- Salt and pepper to taste

Instructions:

1. **Marinate the Shrimp:** In a bowl, combine olive oil, lime juice, honey, chili powder, cayenne pepper, garlic powder, salt, and pepper. Add shrimp and toss to coat. Marinate for 15-30 minutes.
2. **Cook the Shrimp:** Heat a grill or skillet over medium-high heat. Cook the shrimp for 2-3 minutes per side, or until pink and cooked through.
3. **Prepare the Slaw:** In a large bowl, mix shredded cabbage, cilantro, lime juice, honey, salt, and pepper.
4. **Assemble the Tacos:** Warm the tortillas. Place a spoonful of slaw on each tortilla, top with grilled shrimp, and garnish with diced pineapple.
5. **Serve:** Serve immediately, and enjoy!

These tacos offer a delicious combination of spicy shrimp and sweet pineapple!

Grilled Chicken and Mango Salsa Wraps

Ingredients:

For the Grilled Chicken:

- 2 large chicken breasts
- 2 tbsp olive oil
- 1 tbsp lime juice
- 1 tsp ground cumin
- 1 tsp smoked paprika
- 1/2 tsp garlic powder
- 1/2 tsp onion powder
- Salt and pepper to taste

For the Mango Salsa:

- 1 ripe mango, peeled and diced
- 1/2 red bell pepper, diced
- 1/4 red onion, finely chopped
- 1 jalapeño, seeded and finely chopped (optional for heat)
- 2 tbsp fresh cilantro, chopped
- 2 tbsp lime juice
- Salt and pepper to taste

For the Wraps:

- 4 large tortillas (flour or whole wheat)
- 1 cup shredded lettuce or mixed greens
- 1/2 avocado, sliced (optional)

Instructions:

1. **Marinate the Chicken:** In a small bowl, mix olive oil, lime juice, cumin, smoked paprika, garlic powder, onion powder, salt, and pepper. Rub the mixture over the chicken breasts. Marinate for at least 30 minutes.
2. **Grill the Chicken:** Preheat the grill to medium-high heat. Grill chicken breasts for 6-8 minutes per side, or until the internal temperature reaches 165°F (74°C). Let rest for a few minutes, then slice thinly.
3. **Prepare the Mango Salsa:** In a bowl, combine diced mango, red bell pepper, red onion, jalapeño (if using), cilantro, lime juice, salt, and pepper. Mix well.
4. **Assemble the Wraps:** Lay out the tortillas. Place a handful of shredded lettuce or mixed greens in the center of each tortilla. Top with sliced grilled chicken and a generous spoonful of mango salsa. Add avocado slices if desired.

5. **Wrap It Up:** Fold in the sides of the tortilla, then roll it up from the bottom to enclose the filling.
6. **Serve:** Cut the wraps in half if desired, and serve immediately.

Enjoy these vibrant and tasty wraps!

Tropical Chicken and Rice Bowl

Ingredients:

For the Chicken:

- 1 lb chicken breasts or thighs, boneless and skinless
- 2 tbsp olive oil
- 2 tbsp soy sauce
- 2 tbsp pineapple juice
- 1 tbsp honey
- 1 tsp ground ginger
- 1 garlic clove, minced
- Salt and pepper to taste

For the Rice Bowl:

- 2 cups cooked jasmine or basmati rice
- 1 cup fresh pineapple, diced
- 1 red bell pepper, thinly sliced
- 1/2 cucumber, sliced
- 1/4 cup red onion, thinly sliced
- 1 avocado, sliced
- 1/4 cup fresh cilantro, chopped

For the Dressing:

- 1/4 cup soy sauce
- 2 tbsp rice vinegar
- 1 tbsp honey
- 1 tbsp sesame oil
- 1 tsp grated fresh ginger
- 1 garlic clove, minced

Instructions:

1. **Marinate the Chicken:** In a bowl, combine olive oil, soy sauce, pineapple juice, honey, ground ginger, minced garlic, salt, and pepper. Add the chicken and marinate for at least 30 minutes, or up to 4 hours.
2. **Cook the Chicken:** Preheat the grill or a skillet over medium-high heat. Cook the chicken for 5-7 minutes per side, or until fully cooked and the internal temperature reaches 165°F (74°C). Let it rest for a few minutes, then slice into strips.
3. **Prepare the Dressing:** In a small bowl, whisk together soy sauce, rice vinegar, honey, sesame oil, grated ginger, and minced garlic.

4. **Assemble the Rice Bowl:** Divide the cooked rice among bowls. Top with diced pineapple, red bell pepper, cucumber, red onion, and avocado slices. Arrange the sliced chicken on top.
5. **Drizzle and Garnish:** Drizzle with the prepared dressing and sprinkle with fresh cilantro.
6. **Serve:** Enjoy your vibrant and tropical chicken and rice bowl!

This bowl is perfect for a fresh and flavorful meal!

Island-Style Crab Cakes

Ingredients:

For the Chicken:

- 1 lb chicken breasts or thighs, boneless and skinless
- 2 tbsp olive oil
- 2 tbsp soy sauce
- 2 tbsp pineapple juice
- 1 tbsp honey
- 1 tsp ground ginger
- 1 garlic clove, minced
- Salt and pepper to taste

For the Rice Bowl:

- 2 cups cooked jasmine or basmati rice
- 1 cup fresh pineapple, diced
- 1 red bell pepper, thinly sliced
- 1/2 cucumber, sliced
- 1/4 cup red onion, thinly sliced
- 1 avocado, sliced
- 1/4 cup fresh cilantro, chopped

For the Dressing:

- 1/4 cup soy sauce
- 2 tbsp rice vinegar
- 1 tbsp honey
- 1 tbsp sesame oil
- 1 tsp grated fresh ginger
- 1 garlic clove, minced

Instructions:

1. **Marinate the Chicken:** In a bowl, combine olive oil, soy sauce, pineapple juice, honey, ground ginger, minced garlic, salt, and pepper. Add the chicken and marinate for at least 30 minutes, or up to 4 hours.
2. **Cook the Chicken:** Preheat the grill or a skillet over medium-high heat. Cook the chicken for 5-7 minutes per side, or until fully cooked and the internal temperature reaches 165°F (74°C). Let it rest for a few minutes, then slice into strips.
3. **Prepare the Dressing:** In a small bowl, whisk together soy sauce, rice vinegar, honey, sesame oil, grated ginger, and minced garlic.

4. **Assemble the Rice Bowl:** Divide the cooked rice among bowls. Top with diced pineapple, red bell pepper, cucumber, red onion, and avocado slices. Arrange the sliced chicken on top.
5. **Drizzle and Garnish:** Drizzle with the prepared dressing and sprinkle with fresh cilantro.
6. **Serve:** Enjoy your vibrant and tropical chicken and rice bowl!

This bowl is perfect for a fresh and flavorful meal!

Pineapple-Coconut Chicken Salad

Ingredients:

- 2 cups cooked chicken, shredded or diced (grilled or rotisserie chicken works well)
- 1 cup fresh pineapple, diced
- 1/2 cup shredded coconut (toasted or untoasted)
- 1/2 cup red bell pepper, finely diced
- 1/4 cup red onion, finely diced
- 1/4 cup fresh cilantro, chopped
- 2 tbsp lime juice
- 2 tbsp mayonnaise
- 2 tbsp Greek yogurt (or additional mayonnaise)
- 1 tsp honey
- Salt and pepper to taste
- 4 cups mixed greens or lettuce (for serving)

Instructions:

1. **Prepare the Dressing:** In a small bowl, mix together lime juice, mayonnaise, Greek yogurt, honey, salt, and pepper until well combined.
2. **Combine Salad Ingredients:** In a large bowl, combine shredded chicken, diced pineapple, shredded coconut, red bell pepper, red onion, and cilantro.
3. **Add Dressing:** Pour the dressing over the salad mixture and toss gently to coat.
4. **Serve:** Serve the salad on a bed of mixed greens or lettuce.

Enjoy this light and tropical chicken salad!

Caribbean Spiced Chicken Panini

Ingredients:

- 2 boneless, skinless chicken breasts
- 2 tbsp Caribbean jerk seasoning (store-bought or homemade)
- 2 tbsp olive oil
- 4 slices of ciabatta or sourdough bread
- 1/4 cup mayonnaise
- 2 tbsp mango chutney (store-bought or homemade)
- 4 slices of Swiss cheese or your favorite cheese
- 1/2 avocado, sliced
- 1/2 red bell pepper, thinly sliced
- 1/2 small red onion, thinly sliced
- 1 cup fresh spinach or arugula

For Homemade Jerk Seasoning (optional):

- 1 tbsp allspice
- 1 tbsp thyme
- 1 tsp cinnamon
- 1 tsp nutmeg
- 1 tsp paprika
- 1/2 tsp cayenne pepper
- 1 tsp garlic powder
- 1 tsp onion powder
- Salt and pepper to taste

Instructions:

1. **Prepare the Chicken:** Rub the chicken breasts with Caribbean jerk seasoning. Heat olive oil in a skillet over medium-high heat. Cook the chicken breasts for 6-7 minutes per side, or until fully cooked and the internal temperature reaches 165°F (74°C). Let rest for a few minutes, then slice thinly.
2. **Prepare the Spread:** In a small bowl, mix together mayonnaise and mango chutney.
3. **Assemble the Panini:** Spread the mayonnaise-chutney mixture on one side of each slice of bread. On two slices of bread, layer the Swiss cheese, sliced chicken, avocado, red bell pepper, red onion, and spinach. Top with the remaining slices of bread.
4. **Grill the Panini:** Preheat a panini press or a skillet over medium heat. If using a skillet, place a heavy pan on top of the sandwiches to press them down. Grill the sandwiches for 3-4 minutes per side, or until the bread is crispy and golden and the cheese is melted.
5. **Serve:** Slice the paninis in half and serve hot.

Enjoy your Caribbean Spiced Chicken Panini with its vibrant and zesty flavors!

Tropical Fish Tacos with Avocado Sauce

Ingredients:

For the Fish:

- 1 lb firm white fish (like cod, tilapia, or mahi-mahi), cut into strips
- 1/2 cup all-purpose flour
- 1/2 cup cornmeal
- 1 tsp paprika
- 1/2 tsp garlic powder
- 1/2 tsp onion powder
- 1/2 tsp cumin
- 1/2 tsp salt
- 1/4 tsp black pepper
- 1 egg, beaten
- 1 cup breadcrumbs (panko or regular)
- Vegetable oil (for frying)

For the Avocado Sauce:

- 1 ripe avocado
- 1/4 cup Greek yogurt or sour cream
- 2 tbsp lime juice
- 1 clove garlic, minced
- 1/4 cup fresh cilantro, chopped
- Salt and pepper to taste

For the Tacos:

- 8 small tortillas (flour or corn)
- 1 cup shredded cabbage
- 1 cup diced pineapple
- 1/2 red bell pepper, thinly sliced
- Fresh cilantro for garnish (optional)
- Lime wedges for serving

Instructions:

1. **Prepare the Avocado Sauce:** In a blender or food processor, combine avocado, Greek yogurt, lime juice, garlic, cilantro, salt, and pepper. Blend until smooth. Adjust seasoning to taste. Set aside.

2. **Prepare the Fish:** In a shallow dish, mix flour, cornmeal, paprika, garlic powder, onion powder, cumin, salt, and pepper. Place the beaten egg in another shallow dish, and the breadcrumbs in a third dish.
3. **Coat the Fish:** Dredge each fish strip in the flour mixture, then dip in the beaten egg, and coat with breadcrumbs.
4. **Cook the Fish:** Heat vegetable oil in a skillet over medium-high heat. Fry the fish strips for 3-4 minutes per side, or until golden brown and cooked through. Remove from the skillet and drain on paper towels.
5. **Assemble the Tacos:** Warm the tortillas. Place a layer of shredded cabbage on each tortilla, then top with fried fish, diced pineapple, and red bell pepper.
6. **Add Sauce and Garnish:** Drizzle with avocado sauce and garnish with fresh cilantro if desired.
7. **Serve:** Serve the tacos with lime wedges on the side.

Enjoy your tropical fish tacos with their bright and refreshing flavors!

Pineapple and Ginger Chicken Stir-Fry

Ingredients:

- 1 lb chicken breast or thighs, thinly sliced
- 1 cup fresh pineapple, diced
- 2 tbsp vegetable oil
- 1 onion, sliced
- 2 bell peppers (red or yellow), sliced
- 1 cup snap peas or snow peas
- 3 cloves garlic, minced
- 1 tbsp fresh ginger, minced
- 1/4 cup soy sauce
- 2 tbsp hoisin sauce
- 1 tbsp rice vinegar
- 1 tbsp honey
- 1 tbsp cornstarch mixed with 2 tbsp water (for thickening)
- Cooked rice (for serving)
- Sliced green onions and sesame seeds (for garnish, optional)

Instructions:

1. **Prepare the Sauce:** In a small bowl, whisk together soy sauce, hoisin sauce, rice vinegar, and honey. Set aside.
2. **Cook the Chicken:** Heat vegetable oil in a large skillet or wok over medium-high heat. Add the chicken and stir-fry for 4-5 minutes until cooked through. Remove chicken from the skillet and set aside.
3. **Stir-Fry Vegetables:** In the same skillet, add onion, bell peppers, and snap peas. Stir-fry for 3-4 minutes until vegetables are tender-crisp. Add garlic and ginger and cook for an additional 1 minute.
4. **Combine Ingredients:** Return the chicken to the skillet. Pour the sauce over the chicken and vegetables. Stir well to coat everything in the sauce.
5. **Thicken the Sauce:** Stir in the cornstarch mixture and cook for another 1-2 minutes until the sauce has thickened.
6. **Add Pineapple:** Gently fold in the diced pineapple and cook for an additional 1-2 minutes until heated through.
7. **Serve:** Serve the stir-fry over cooked rice and garnish with sliced green onions and sesame seeds if desired.

Enjoy your flavorful and tropical chicken stir-fry!